Trump's
Counter-Revolution

Trump's
Counter-Revolution

Mikkel Bolt Rasmussen

Winchester, UK
Washington, USA

First published by Zero Books, 2018
Zero Books is an imprint of John Hunt Publishing Ltd., No. 3 East St., Alresford,
Hampshire SO24 9EE, UK
office1@jhpbooks.net
www.johnhuntpublishing.com
www.zero-books.net

For distributor details and how to order please visit the 'Ordering' section on our website.

Text copyright: Mikkel Bolt Rasmussen 2017

ISBN: 978 1 78904 018 0
978 1 78904 019 7 (ebook)
Library of Congress Control Number: 2018934827

A CIP catalogue record for this book is available from the British Library.

Design: Stuart Davies

Printed and bound by CPI Group (UK) Ltd, Croydon, CR0 4YY, UK
US: Printed and bound by Edwards Brothers Malloy 15200 NBN Way #B, Blue Ridge Summit,
PA 17214, USA.

We operate a distinctive and ethical publishing philosophy in
all areas of our business, from our global network of authors to
production and worldwide distribution.

Contents

Also by the author

After the Great Refusal
Essays on Contemporary Art, Its Contradictions and Difficulties
Zero Books, 2018
ISBN: 978-1-78535-758-9

Introduction

The purpose of this small book is twofold. Firstly, it analyzes the meaning of Trump as a late-capitalist fascism that solves the economic crisis by returning to an imagined idea of a national community through protectionism and nationalist measures. Secondly, it criticizes the opposition between Trump and democracy that has been a staple of liberal discourse since Trump's election. Trump is a problem, but the solution is not to defend a dysfunctional parliamentary national democracy. Instead, I suggest that Trump is the symptom of fundamental problems in a shrinking capitalist economy that is unable to integrate its proletarians.

The book has four parts. In the first, I analyze Trump's election as a 'protest' against neoliberal globalization and its different policies of outsourcing, deregulation, privatization and cuts in welfare. The financial crisis of 2008 made visible this 30-year-long development and called it into question, but without formulating any real alternatives to the status quo. Instead, the crisis, the bailout of the banks, and the ensuing cuts and foreclosures resulted in a dramatic rise in discontent that manifested itself in a rise in nationalism. In Europe, Brexit is one example of this development. Trump is an American response. Trump channels the 'abandoned' white working-class's discontent and is promising a national solution to the crisis. His plan is to turn around the continued drop in the global economy though protectionism, deregulation and public investments.

Trump's election is thus a protest against neoliberal globalization. But Trump is also a protest against the protests. Trump is to be understood as a response to an emerging rejection, not only of the current regime of accumulation but also of capitalism as a mode of production. The Arab revolutions, the square occupation movement and Black Lives Matter constitute the coming into being of a new global protest movement. I argue that Trump is the ultra-nationalist response to these protests. An attempt to derail them and prevent them from articulating an alternative. In that sense, Trump is a counter-revolutionary solution, where protests against the last 3 decades of internationalization and de-regulation and the last 10 years of austerity politics is steered in a fascist direction with ideas of a chosen people led by a strong leader. 'Make America great again'.

In the second part of the book I show how Trump is the final confirmation of the transformation of politics into image politics. Political messages and campaigns are not just put into images but emerge as genuine image events. Trump understands this and his crazy Twitter comments against the 'lying and dishonest' media, 'weak' politicians and 'so-called' judges use codes from the pop-cultural industries and transform them into a 'political' programme. It does therefore not make sense to try and prove that Trump is lying or contradicting himself. His politics is a virtual politics that is purposefully self-contradictory, silly and violent.

We are confronted with a strange disruption in slow motion, in which former certainties dissolve, but without being replaced by new ones. The ideological dominance of the neoliberal order has been broken, but the local elites have not been able to come up with something new and have great difficulties adapting to the new situation. Trump is a temporary solution that simultaneously promises to continue the neoliberal programme, but also increases neoliberalism's racist solutions, thereby giving them an explicitly fascist dimension. The programme is the re-establishment of a fictive former greatness, where the white male reigned unchallenged. Trump's racism, misogyny and Islamophobia are the ingredients of a postmodern fascism that uses systematic lies and attacks on the mainstream press, ultra-nationalism and the mobilization of an outraged white petty bourgeoisie.

In the third section, I analyze Trump's inauguration speech

on 20 January 2017. In his speech, Trump narrates a story about the decline of the USA. The political elite has allowed huge masses of migrants to enter the country. But Trump will set things straight and restore order. Trump is the strong leader that will build a great wall and kick out the foreigners. It is not the USA Trump talks about, but America. 'Make America great again'. 'America' is an imaginary community that does not include the people that make up the United States, but all the 'real' Americans, meaning the white Americans. Trump promises to hand back power to its righteous owners. He employs several historical references from discourses of social-Darwinist whiteness, in which the white capitalist class and the white working class are the only genuine Americans. Blacks, Latinos and Native Americans are not part of this community. Trump is constantly talking about all the things that threaten his imagined America and that he is ready to implement 'radical new solutions' to protect it.

Finally, I explain that although Trump is to be analyzed as a kind of pastiche fascism, we should not defend democracy against Trump. Trump is not a populist who has performed a kind of democratic coup, using democracy undemocratically. Trump is immanent to national democracy. He is the expression of a crisis in democracy, where it becomes necessary to further activate the exclusions already present in national parliamentary democracy. He is not some kind of external threat, but a product of the democratic system itself. He makes visible those operations that often remain invisible in the West, but that are present all the time. The treatment of migrants in Europe today is a case in point. In the US, the control and shooting of African Americans by the police is the best example. The repressive apparatus of the state is being put to use in a more straightforward way now. Today, we all live in the post colony.

The book puts three connected concepts to use in the analysis of Trump: counter-revolution, fascism and image politics. In my reading, Trump is to be understood as a fascist counter-revolution that is derailing the coming into being of real capital-negating alternatives to neoliberal globalization. In a situation of deep economic crisis that has become a political crisis and is starting to become a crisis for the state, Trump's American fascism offers an unstable solution, in which racism and protectionism are combined in a strange postmodern fascism. The answer is neither to oppose Trump and democracy, nor to engage in antifascism in favour of political democracy and political rights. Political democracy is no doubt a lesser evil than Trump's late-capitalist fascism, but it is an evil nonetheless. And an evil that made possible the election of Trump and his racist and exclusionary policies. National democracy is slowly transforming itself into fascism. The capitalist crisis necessitates this move. In a systemic crisis, as in the one we are living through now, the political form of capitalism can shift from democracy to fascism. The most important thing is to protect property rights, enhance the interests of big capital and control the proletarians, who are unable to enter the metabolism of capital. There is thus no opposition between liberal democracy and fascism. The differences between these two political forms are less important than the similarities. The task must be to establish the possibility of a critique of both fascism and national democracy, in favour of a different post-capitalist organization of the world. What this is to look like remains unclear. Right now, it is the abolition of national democracy and its immanent fascist possibility that we have to focus on.

Throughout the text, I use terms and concepts from the revolutionary tradition, left communism, the Situationists and different subsequent Marxist or post-Marxist philosophers. In the endnotes, I refer to the most important ones. I have limited the number of references to a minimum and am freely using this imaginary party's vocabulary. The book has my name on the cover but is, of course, the result of a collective praxis. I am grateful to a long list of people, most notably James Day, Peer Illner, Carsten Juhl and Katarina Stenbeck.

Chapter 1

A Protest against the Protests

What had seemed unthinkable became reality. Donald J Trump first gained the Republican nomination, and then beat Hillary Clinton in the US presidential election in the fall of 2016. Thus, President Trump replaced President Obama in January 2017. Obama, America's first black president and recipient of the Nobel Peace Prize (but also, of course, the keen user of drone warfare, the banks' saviour and deporter of illegal immigrants). The eloquent, humorous and dialogue-seeking Obama was succeeded by Trump, who had never held public office, but made his name as a flamboyant property speculator, proprietor of bankrupt casinos and more recently, star of his own reality show, *The Apprentice*. Until he ran for president, Trump's most noticeable contribution to American political life had been his dogged insistence that Obama wasn't American. The contrast between the out-going president and his successor could not have been greater. Trump's victory over Clinton took many by surprise, since all the mainstream media, from CNN and NBC to the *New York Times* and the *Washington Post* had warned strongly of the dangers of a Trump presidency. If this wasn't enough, pretty much all the diplomatic, military, cultural and political establishment, including a large part of the Republican Party, whom Trump represented, sought to distance themselves from him. But to no avail; Trump won just enough votes to win the election and became president. Clinton won the most votes, 2.7 million more, but Trump won the most electors and therefore won the election.

The mobilization against Trump was spectacular. It's rare that neo-conservative commentators and left-wing activists have struggled side by side, as they did against Trump. All the politico-economic mainstream and its media in the USA and Western Europe, the *Economist*, *Financial Times* and the *Guardian*, along with *Børsen* and *Politikken* in Denmark, *Le Monde* and *Le Figaro* in France, and *Frankfurter Allgemeine* and *Süddeutsche Zeitung* in Germany, agitated more and more strongly against 'The Donald'. As did the rest of the Left in the USA and Western Europe, anti-racists, LBGTQ groups, campaigners for social justice and human-rights organizations. All were united against Trump. In Denmark, former Prime Minister and ex Security General of NATO, Anders Fogh Rasmussen, warned of the possibility of global recession in the case of a Trump presidency, and Johanne Schmidt-Nielsen, former spokesperson for the red-green alliance Enhedslisten, was shaken by Trump's campaign. Everyone was frightened at the prospect of the blonde, fake-tanned building matador sitting in the Oval Office. Few thought it possible that he would win. But as we know only too well, that's nevertheless exactly what happened.

In hindsight, there were many signs pointing in that direction. Not least the vote for Brexit in Great Britain. The status quo is only maintained with the utmost difficulty at the moment. Matteo Renzi's inability to push through constitutional reform in Italy shortly after his victory was the next example of dissolution. On the same day in December 2016, Norbert Hofer was just about prevented from becoming President of Austria after a nip and tuck race, but it seems fair to say there's a pattern here. Although Marine Le Pen 'only' progressed to the second round of the French presidential election and lost to Macron, the underlying pattern is painfully clear: the ruling order has great difficulties reproducing itself, giving ground to a rapidly accelerating turn to the right.

This is the story of Trump as part of something much larger, the current high point in a rapidly growing rejection of the political system as we have known it since the fall of the Berlin Wall. Populations defy the media and experts' expectations and vote against the 'system', and therefore vote the 'wrong' way. All across the world, people are reacting to a situation characterized by dissolution and crisis, in which the established political parties are seen as out of touch and unable to change course or offer something else.

The effect of Trump's victory is political chaos. The Republicans are at sixes and sevens and, up to now, are deeply split over Trump as their president. Not only do they now control both Senate and Congress, they also have a majority in the Supreme Court and, most importantly, they have the presidency. But, Speaker of the House of Representatives Paul Ryan and Trump disagree on a whole range of signature policies. Things look much worse for the Democrats, though; the party managed to lose an election against the least likely of all candidates and many now hope that the party will collapse so that new ones can be formed, not so attached to the political and economic interests that the Clintons represented.

An initial analysis of the election of Trump would be that he encapsulates the recent popular reaction. Trump is anything but mainstream. He is not only a rejection of the politics broadly accepted by mainstream economists and established politicians, he's also a break with the previous US political system. Right enough he stood as a Republican candidate, but he was in open conflict with more or less all the party's leading members and, during the election campaign, made more out of the similarity between the Democratic and Republican parties as corrupt members of the political establishment under the sway of the banks. Washington had been lining its own pockets and couldn't give a damn about ordinary Americans was a common soundbite. In this way, Trump emerged as a protest against the system. He came from the outside and dissolved the opposition between Democrats and Republicans that had dominated the political system since the middle of the nineteenth century. Trump held this binary structure in suspense and, even though he made use of one of the big parties, he wasn't like any of the other candidates, who were all experienced politicians. He was a mix between Robin Hood and Citizen Kane, at one and the same time a man of the people fighting a corrupt elite, and a self-made man who had founded a business empire and was now moving into politics.

Trump stood out, then, as a rejection of the norm. His election is an expression of protest. Many of those who voted Trump said they didn't especially like him, but they were sick and tired of politicians and the political system, and this is why they were voting Trump. Trump refused to accept the conventional code of conduct during his campaign, and at no point laid out anything near a coherent political programme. Any idea of politics as a knowledgeable dialogue, based on a well-informed argument was replaced by violent tirades against migrants, Muslims, black criminals, Wall Street and the government. And that's what worked. Trump was different, he wasn't reasonable, but tasteless. He was a latter-day Jesse James, who took the fight to the establishment and its naturalized values.

As remarked earlier, Trump is part of something bigger. Phenomenon Trump can't be explained away as an American thing. It's important, of course, to look closely at voting patterns and the distribution of votes among specific groups of the population, which parts of American society voted for whom and how this compares with previous elections, but we also have to extend analysis to articulate the relationship between Trump's election and similar events elsewhere (it's not just a question of identity politics, right or left). In other words, we have to account for the context, which is the political and economic history of 2008 or, as we will see, since the beginning of the 1970s. As English historian Perry Anderson writes in *Le Monde diplomatique*, Trump is part of the anti-system protest on the right that is spreading across the world at the moment.[1] The US election should be understood in the framework of a global scenario of tumultuous change, where authoritarian right-wing radical movements challenge the so-called neoliberal elite and move into the corridors of power. Trump takes his place alongside authoritarian leaders like General al-Sisi in Egypt, Recep Erdogan in Turkey, Narendra Modi in India, Rodrigo Duterte in the Philippines, Mauricio Macri in Argentina and Michel Temer in Brazil, and, of course, his Russian friend, Vladimir Putin. Europe hasn't been passed by either. Here we have Viktor Orban in power in Hungary, the party Law and Justice in Poland, led by Jaroslaw Aleksander Kaczynski, and Milos Zeman in the Czech Republic. This is one of the paradoxes right now: the anti-system forces seem to appear under the banner of nationalism and incarnate a hard-core nationalist agenda. The challenge to the status quo comes from the right. In the North, Norway and, most of all, Denmark have been advanced countries in the current right turn, as explicitly Islamophobic parties have turned Islamophobia into government policy. There are, of course, important differences between the various politicians and parties across the globe, but they all draw on a xenophobic nationalism that breaks with 50 years dominated by the discourse of human rights, however real or imagined this may have been institutionally and geopolitically. In the wealthy North, racism is expressed more jovially (like in the cartoons depicting Muhammad in *Jyllands-Posten* in 2005), while in the global South, it takes on much more obviously authoritarian dimensions. But the development is the same. As they say in France, the 1930s are before us again.

Crisis

The backdrop to this development is a politicization of the economic crisis, which simply seems to continue and therefore rub off on asylum policy. Trump is an attempt to nationalize a way out of the crisis, politically and economically, politically through white supremacy and economically through protectionism and command economy.

That we find ourselves in a period of crisis is undeniable.

Hence the uncertain and rudderless way of governing. The ruling classes have a hard time reproducing their hegemony, and neoliberal politics has suffered an ideological defeat that it doesn't seem able to recover from. There isn't really anything that works like it did before. Neither investment nor austerity, the economy just won't get going again, and it's hard to foresee which direction things take. Received modes of thought have shown their limits, but at the same time no new ones seem available. What's going on? Are we simply confronted with so-called secular stagnation, as economist Paul Krugman hopes, or are we confronted with a fundamental crisis of the capitalist system, as world-systems theorist Immanuel Wallerstein argues? Whatever the case, much points to the end of the short American century.[2] The value crisis is so encompassing that the USA is struggling to turn things around.

The financial crisis is, of course, a crucial factor, but phenomena like the geopolitical instability after 9/11 and the invasions of Afghanistan and Iraq, the wave of protests in 2011, the growing movement of people and the climate crisis are also part of the mix. They are all tendencies that challenge national economics and put pressure on the established political system, not least in the USA. People react by abandoning the old parties and by looking elsewhere. Thus, Trump as protest.

And there are links between Trump's victory and the financial crisis, which revealed the rampant inequality at the heart of the US economy. As documentary director Michael Moore, but also the left communist journal *Insurgent Notes* explain, the election of Trump is a rebellion against a 25-year-long intense neoliberal globalization, where outsourcing and deindustrialization have slowly eaten away at the customary way of life of a large part of the American working and middle classes.[3] A relationship which first became visible with a slight delay, however, because a growing credit economy kept the Western working class afloat for a number of years, but in 2008 the bubble burst, and suddenly working-class families had to hold down three or four jobs in order to survive, or borrow heavily to keep a roof over their heads and give their kids an education. This is the socio-economic cause of Trump's success: a fall in real wages, economic uncertainty and unemployment. Conditions that the ruling class has had a hard time taking seriously, even after the financial crisis, where politicians chose to bail out the banks and socialize the costs of the burst credit bubble.

So the backdrop to Trump is the financial crisis, which broke out in 2007/8 in the USA and quickly developed into an economic crisis, which spread across the world, but hit the USA and Europe especially hard. Governments dealt with the crisis, just as Mussolini had in the 1930s. They took on the banks' debts and then cut deep into the remnants of the welfare state that had survived 3 decades of neoliberal restructuring. The crisis thus developed into a real political crisis. The ruling classes just carried on as if nothing had happened. The representatives of the current ruling class were unable to see the problem with their political agenda. Inequality grew explosively, globally and locally, and more and more workers were thrown off the labour market, which resulted in growing unrest. Saving the very institutions which were responsible for the finance bubble in the first place was the priority. The immediate reaction to the popped housing and credit bubbles, which spread from the USA to the rest of the world, was to give the banks, insurance companies and finance capitals an enormous amount of money in order to stop them from going bankrupt. This operation revealed the inflated economy's odd mechanics, in which paper money is printed without any connection to the production of value. Their deficits suddenly vanished and the banks went on as if nothing had happened. Nation states had taken on their debt, leaving most countries even deeper in the red than they already were. The alliance between political leaders and finance capital was all of a sudden very clear. Bill and Hillary Clinton are obvious examples of this alliance, and their close connections with Goldman Sachs and Wall Street without doubt worked against Hillary in the eyes of many voters. The banks were saved, while many Americans were driven out of house and home.

The outbreak of the financial crisis and its subsequent management revealed some of the underlying tendencies that had gone more or less unnoticed for a long time. Not least the cavernous inequality of income distribution in countries like the USA, where the richest part of the population had cut itself an increasingly large slice of the cake.

As we know from the Marxist historian Robert Brenner, the problem is that the production of surplus value hasn't increased for a good while. Since the end of the 1960s, the global economy and the economies of the advanced capitalist countries, not least the USA, experienced a significant drop in the rate of profit, while at the same time the richest part of the population has grown richer and richer.[4] This development is the result of the neoliberal politics that have set the agenda since the beginning of the 1980s, and which have been a political attempt to compensate for the decline in value creation by transferring large sums to the rich through tax cuts, deregulation and other such initiatives.

As Brenner has shown, what we are confronted with is a longer history dating back to the end of the Second World War. The economies in the USA and Western Europe went like the clappers for a 25-year period after the war, but ran out of steam at the end of the 1960s. The advanced capitalist economies have been trapped in a slow decline of lower growth, increasing inequality and repeated crises ever since. Neoliberalism was an answer to this crisis. As there was less to distribute, Reagan, Thatcher and little by little all other politicians in the Western world, and after 1989, in Eastern Europe too, correlatively pushed through not only extensive tax cuts, which benefited the rich, but also cracked down on trade unions. The goal was to weaken the workers and prevent them from getting a greater part of the value they produce. This is the history of neoliberalism as an answer to 1968, and as an attempt to splinter the core of worker militancy in the USA and Western Europe and replace them with cheaper wage slaves elsewhere, not least in China, since the country's economy was opened at the end of the 1970s. In retrospect it is obvious that so-called neoliberalism wasn't an effective long-term solution. Or rather, it was, of course; an enormous concentration of wealth has taken place in the last 30 years, but the money economy's underlying problems haven't been solved. This is why Marxist economists talk of neoliberalism as a slow crash landing, where capitalism's been running on empty for the last 30 years, and where inconceivable amounts of credit have been the primary force driving growth. The enormous growth in international trade, in the movement of capital and on the stock markets made it look as though the economy was doing alright, it looked as though profit and the production of value were independent of each other, as though the process of accumulation had freed itself from the process of production. Only of course it hadn't. Just as manual labour hadn't disappeared, as some sociologists and philosophers believed it had for a while. No, history hadn't come to an end, and the neoliberal economy didn't create growth, but an enormous amount of paper money that gave the illusion of growth. Paper money endowed the period with the gloss of normality, though all the while there were crises. There was crisis at the beginning of the 1970s, at the beginnings of the 1980s and 1990s, the beginning of the 2000s and again from 2007 and on. If we look at the neoliberal era from the perspective of social reproduction, it almost takes on the character of a 30-year war, in which neoliberalism attacks the working class relentlessly. But it was a Pyrrhic victory; rejection of the working class wasn't enough to lift the rate of profit, even though it looked for a good while as if credit and revenues from shares were the solution.

That stopped in its tracks in 2007, when the global bubble

burst and revealed piles of bad debt, which had kept the economy afloat. Suddenly it became clear that a thoroughgoing and irreversible deindustrialization had taken place in the heartlands of capitalism, as part of the incorporation of more and more workers on a global scale had made it possible to reduce costs and break the mulish workers in the West, who, since the 1960s, had 'misunderstood' the post-war wage-productivity deal and demanded more than mere access to consumer goods and the welfare state. For part of the Western working class, neoliberal restructuring took the form of permanent unemployment and an explosion of precarious, low-income jobs. For a while, this development was held in abeyance thanks to the many and various ways of taking on debt. But that grew increasingly difficult after the crisis. The neoliberal crash landing had already long since undermined working-class identity, but now the collapse became especially obvious, and suddenly workers in the West found themselves cast out of the economy, and the youth in the South and North held their stolen futures in common. This was the background to the global wave of protests that rolled across in 2010 and 2011, but it was also the backdrop to Trump's election victory.

Even though the financial crisis did not result in a change of course politically – the political elite seemed unable to look critically at a doctrine which had taken on the status of a self-evident truth – things shifted. Suddenly, the 30-year long spread of neoliberal accumulation, where savings were made in reproduction and labour power, became visible. Rampant inequality was suddenly not simply an image of the USA as the land of opportunity, but a problem.

The protests

As it became increasingly clear that the main job facing the changing governments in the USA and Europe in the wake of the financial crisis was shoring up the economy with complete disregard for the people's dearth, something began to happen. It started in Southern Europe, where the crisis was used to press through extensive cuts, which aimed at getting countries like Greece, Spain and Portugal, and to a lesser degree Italy, to follow the same economic policy as the rest of Europe. The result was obvious: recession and therefore unemployment, falling wages and social unrest. National governments were forced into humiliating deals with the IMF and European Central Bank, without their people having any real say in the matter. Things were especially garish in Greece, where neo-Eurocommunist SYRIZA came to power in the wake of widespread resistance to the loan packages, but who nevertheless had to accept the same kind of deal a short time after their victory, without managing to negotiate so much as a comma. This situation showed that the distance between parliament and street was unbridgeable, and the state in reality functioned as an instrument of domination. There wasn't even much of a political tussle about it; SYRIZA couldn't change the hand they were dealt and were engaged in an impossible project from the start.

At the turn of the year 2010/11, people in Athens, Madrid and Lisbon began protesting against the austerity programmes. The protests grew rapidly, and in no time turned into actual movements, which counted participants by the thousand. At the same time, revolution broke out in Tunisia and Egypt, where rising bread prices had caused discontent to boil over. After decades of seeing local potentates, supported by the West, enrich themselves, something clicked, and in just a few weeks the Tunisian and Egyptian revolutions succeeded in overthrowing Ben Ali and Murbarak. The revolts quickly spread to pretty much all the countries across North Africa and the Middle East, and in no time there was civil war in Libya, Syria and Yemen. Questions were suddenly asked of the postcolonial world order and its neocolonialism, clientism and underdevelopment. The Egyptian revolutionaries occupied Tahrir Square in Cairo, and the tactic inspired protest movements in Europe to follow suit, taking over central squares in many European cities. First in Greece, Spain and Portugal, but not long after in Italy and then most Northern European countries.[5]

Resistance flared up in the United States too, and in September 2011, demonstrators occupied Zuccotti Park in Manhattan to protest against growing inequality and the government bail out of the banks. There had already been a more limited, but nevertheless remarkable, confrontation in 2009, when students at the University of California protested against a hike in tuition fees. In the summer of 2011, thousands of public sector workers occupied the Wisconsin State Capitol in Madison to protest against a ban on collective bargaining. However, it was first with Occupy Wall Street that something more serious happened in the USA. With slogans like 'Down with the tyranny of finance capital' and 'We are the 99%', the demonstrators pointed to the enormous inequality in the USA, where the richest 0.1 per cent owned 35.6 per cent of value, while the poorest 68.4 per cent only have 4.2 per cent. Occupy Wall Street spread like wildfire, and there were soon occupations in hundreds of cities across the country, predominantly up and down the coasts. The youth in the big cities took over privatized squares, protested by reclaiming public space and used it as a stage experiment with egalitarian politics. As social protest on this scale hadn't been seen in the USA since the beginning of the 1970s, Occupy came as a genuine surprise for many.

After more than 30 years of 'one-sided' class struggle, a hole was suddenly cut through 'capitalist realism'.[6] Occupy was a rediscovery of earlier types of militancy and anti-capitalist resistance, but the protests fell apart relatively quickly. The period from September to December 2011 was its highpoint, and the level of activity fell exponentially over the following months. Following 30 years of intense neoliberal individualization, it was hard to recreate a language that could articulate a coherent critique of the system beyond moralism and single-issue activism, while at the same time the FBI and local police did what they could to keep a lid on the protests. The occupation of Zuccotti Park was cleared several times and many were arrested and given a bruising by the police.

In March 2012, in the wake of Occupy's collapse, a new protest movement arose, Black Lives Matter, in which African Americans protested against a racist police force that shoots young black men, but also against America's 'white' capitalism, which excludes African Americans from the economy. American capitalism produces racial inequality, which means that many black lives are superfluous for capitalism, they don't make up a reserve army, they're just left over. The police have the job of keeping this surplus population at bay, the poor have to be kept down. The police's role is thus to keep a check on those workers who can't sell their labour power. This is the socio-economic context of police violence. Racism and de-industrialization melt together in a brutal cocktail that makes African Americans objects for what Frank B. Wilderson calls gratuitous violence.[7] African Americans are simply worth less than others and are therefore far more susceptible to becoming subjects of police violence. The statistics are disquieting: every 28 hours the police shoot a black man in America. This, coupled with the number of black prisoners – African Americans make up 13 per cent of the US populace, but 40 per cent of its prison population – gives an image outline of institutionalized racism. A total of 6 per cent of African Americans between the ages of 30-39 are in jail, compared with only 1 per cent of the white population, and the chances of ending up behind bars are five times greater if you're black. There are, then, more black men sitting in jail than going to college today, and if you're black, you're 30 per cent more likely to be stopped by the police than if you're white.[8]

Because of the structural transformations that have taken place in the economy since the 1970s, many of those who have been classified black haven't been able to find work and therefore have been forced to survive as best they can. They are excluded from the civil rights movement 'American Dream' and have to survive in poverty and crime. Some have been able to borrow, others have been out in jail. The struggle for rights in the 1960s – 'I have a dream' – created an image of a post-racial America, where African Americans are even able to become president, but the tradition of police violence tells another story, where a disproportionately large number of people, who can't get by, are designated black and exposed to racism. More than 2 centuries of slavery and nearly 100 years' lack of political rights live on in the form of material inequality, which only a lucky few African Americans can overcome. The overwhelming majority are simply left to get by with the little they have. This is the ordinary function of capitalism; the poor stay poor.

The combination of racist repression and capitalist exclusion is the backdrop to Black Lives Matter, which first saw the light of day in March 2012 following the killing of 17-year-old Trayvon Martin. Martin was shot by a white security guard, who wasn't even arrested at first, and, when the public prosecutor was eventually pressed into making a case against him, found not guilty. Martin was just one tragic instance in a long list of killings of young African Americans. In November 2012 Jordan Davis, also 17, was shot at a gas station because he wouldn't turn the music in his car down, and in 2013, Renisha McBride was shot as she asked for help after a traffic accident. Demonstrations were already taking place in 2012 and 2013, but it was first in the aftermath of the killing of Michael Brown in Ferguson in August 2014 that there was mass mobilization against police violence. After things had spilled onto the streets, the situation became a matter of national concern, which politicians and the mainstream media were forced to pay attention to. Brown, aged 18, who was unarmed, was shot 12 times by a white police man following a robbery, in which Brown had stolen cigarettes from a corner shop. Unrest broke out in Ferguson the following day with confrontations between the police and outraged African Americans. The protests went on for more than a week, shops were plundered and cars and petrol stations burned. The police response was heavy-handed. Not seeking to calm the unrest, they drove into the memorial, where the Brown family had lain flowers only the day after the killing, and thereafter deployed a large part of the military hardware, which they, like many other state police departments, had invested in as part of the War on Terror. The police, reinforced by the National Guard, fired tear gas, smoke bombs, flash grenades and rubber bullets into the crowd. They were no longer in the usual blue uniforms, but in battle dress, heavily armed with machine guns mounted on armoured cars, not unlike those used in Iraq and Afghanistan. A no-fly zone was put in place over the city, and the police scrambled helicopters to quell the unrest.

In November 2017, a grand jury decided that no charges should be pressed against the officer who shot Brown. The decision led to wide-ranging protest and unrest in the streets, not only in Ferguson, but across more than 100 US cities. The list of murdered young black men is getting longer and longer, and in April 2015 there was more violent unrest, when 25-year-old Freddie Gray died from spinal injuries, suffered while in police custody. He had been taken away by the police and bundled into the back of a police van with his hands and feet bound, and went into a coma during the journey. The event resulted in demonstrations and rioting on the streets of Baltimore and other American cities. The six police officers involved in Gray's death were either acquitted or not brought to trial at all during the summer and fall of 2016.

Like Occupy, Black Lives Matter is a large, composite protest movement, which includes many different agendas, from concrete proposals for better training for the police, or requiring that officers wear body cameras, to revolutionary demands for the abolition of racist capitalism. By drawing on the civil rights movement in the 1960s, Black Lives Matter has formulated demands for institutional reform, but also put forward demands for economic compensation for slavery. Others have pointed out that only more radical structural transformation will alter the living conditions of those hit hardest by the effects of a crisis-ridden capitalism. The problem is not the individual cop's racism, but the social system in which people earmarked 'black' are exposed to structural violence and exclusion. In the last instance, the problem, of course, is capitalism itself, a system in which money begets money without respect for people or the planet's biosphere.

When speaking about Black Lives Matter during the election campaign, Trump didn't beat around the bush; for him, it was a question of protecting police officers from black criminals. Instead of Black Lives Matter, he suggested 'Blue Lives Matter', it was the police who were the victims, they were assaulted by black criminals and were inadequately supported by politicians locally and nationally. According to Trump, Black Lives Matter had declared 'war against police officers'. While the number of cases of violence against the police is the lowest in 25 years, this didn't stop Trump from talking of a 'dangerous anti-police atmosphere', which his government would fight with all the means at their disposal. There's no doubt about it for Trump. The problem isn't police racism, it isn't actually a problem if the police are racist. The problem is black criminals, but especially Black Lives Matter, who must therefore be fought off actively. And legislation has already gone through at state level after Trump was sworn in, laws that give the police even greater powers and further criminalize anti-police violence, including making assault on a police officer a hate crime. The point is simple enough; as it stood on the White House's homepage the day after Trump became president, 'Our job is not to make life more comfortable for the rioter, the looter, or the violent disrupter.' Much stronger punitive measures must therefore be put in place, for example cracking down on resisting arrest. And Trump will allow the police to buy heavy weapons again, which had only been limited after the trouble in Ferguson. The battle lines are being drawn very clearly.

In combination, Occupy and Black Lives Matter make up the first serious challenge to American capitalism in 40 years. Trump is a violent answer to this challenge. The fear of radical change brings fascist solutions into play. American capitalism's problems run deep and it's time for another kettle of fish.

We are dealing with a process of discontinuous dissolution, in which one conflict replaces another in a run of events, riddled with contradictions, in which revolutionary tendencies are constantly derailed or repressed. This is the context of Trump's election victory. With Trump, a mobilization of the 'forgotten' and overlooked arrived in the small towns of middle America. If Occupy was the youth in New York and California, and Black Lives Matter was the black population, then Trump's supporters are the white and blue-collar workers outside of the metropolis, who reject the last 30 years of economic restructuring and demand the restitution of the previous (white) welfare of a previous era. After Occupy, Trump, we might say.

Counter-revolution

There is thus a clear counter-revolutionary element to Trump. Taken together, Occupy and Black Lives Matter are the sign of a nascent reckoning with a racist capitalist system.[9] Trump is a markedly national-capitalist answer, which the white and middle classes respond to as they resolutely reject any fundamental break with their privileged access to wage labour. The logic seems to be, the jobs that are still in the USA are the prerogative of whites. Thus, 45 per cent of white women voted Trump in an attempt to guarantee themselves and their offspring a first pick on jobs and consumer goods. Understood this way, Trump is anything but a break, but rather a desperate extension of a white American democracy under pressure. We have now reached a stage at which the world market has reached the limits of possible expansion and is replaced by national, conservative protection of the internal market. The counter-revolution is being organized.

Trump is thus a protest against the protests, a highly violent swatting away of demands for another world. Instead, the USA will return to the good old days, when the white man was the unchallenged master. Things have been brought into disorder, and Trump will restore the natural order of things. Women, blacks and all other subalterns will be out in their place. This is what 'Make America great again' really means. National community is like a family, with pere Trump at the head of the table. President Trump is a domestic tyrant, who chucks all the recalcitrant blacks in jail, grabs hysterical white women by the crotch and bombs Muslims.

The crisis forces capital to disregard the cosmopolitan rhetoric of freedom of movement and democracy, prevalent in the 1990s. Things need tightening up, and a revival of fascism appears as a solution, fusing racism, sexism and Islamophobia with pop-culture trash talking and idiocy. Trump's counter-revolution is not only a question of hindering the resistance which Occupy and Black Lives Matter mobilized, it's also an attempt to put the skids on any autonomous revolutionary potential well into the future, even if this means giving up on certain customary ideas of tolerance and openness.

If, then, Trump is an expression of protest, we're talking about a counter protest, a response to a genuine, systemic critique that Trump, and the nationalist faction of the capitalist class that supports him, want for all the world to prevent from getting the wind in their sails. It's about circumventing Black Lives Matter's critique of structural racism being coupled to a critique of American capitalism and the capitalist mode of production as a whole.

While Trump is a blank rejection of Black Lives Matter, he's a partial recuperation of Occupy's critique of the financial crisis and bail out of the banks. Trump draws on the critique of neoliberal globalization that Occupy articulated, but puts a completely different spin on it. While he lashes out at Wall Street – he'll allow the banks a free hand notwithstanding and has already sought to initiate big tax cuts for business – but really has the knives out for the previous government, which, according to him, has let American jobs disappear to Mexico, China and other places. He nimbly succeeded in establishing a cross-class alliance between select 'victims' of the financial crisis, namely the white middle class, and protectionist capitalists. The latter are, of course, like Trump, completely indifferent to the growing inequality – Trump seldom talks about wages, for example – but complain about how difficult it is to make profit. It's here that Trump comes into the picture: he canalizes white middle-class fear of social decline and draws together the growing dissatisfaction among part of the capitalist class with the current regime of accumulation. Trump therefore becomes a critic of deindustrialization and neoliberal globalization. The problem, of course, is that Trump short circuits the analysis and points to specific actors as enemies of the American people. It's Washington that's the villain. China's the enemy. It's Mexican immigrants who are stealing our jobs. It's Europe that's to blame for the slump. There is, then, a short-circuited critique of neoliberalism out and about with Trump, where what in reality are systemic faults or structural historical changes are identified as concrete problems that can be eradicated through protectionist exclusion.

Washington, migrant workers, trade deals and supranational organizations are the problem and return to the homeland the answer. A state-backed national economy can, according to Trump and his cohort, rein in globalization. The project is thus to re-establish national sovereignty politically and economically.

A reactionary nationalism or new fascism is the way forward. A strong state that cracks down on unrest, while simultaneously commencing large construction projects, which can get people into work. The dream is that the crisis of American industrial capitalism can be overcome by building up the national economy, provoking trade wars and excluding 'aliens'.

Neoliberalism

Trump's part-adoption of a critique of neoliberalism shows the limitations of such a critique. When such otherwise eminent philosophers and commentators as Mike Davis, Nancy Fraser and Naomi Klein reduce Trump's election victory to a narrative about how the Democratic Party has not only promoted, but been thoroughly dependant on global finance capital, they repeat not only a very short, but also racist history of 'neoliberal decline', which we can overcome if we return to the working-class politics of days of yore, as represented by Bernie Sanders.[10] Trump was the right's, and Sanders the left's, uprising against neoliberal globalization, according to their analysis. The problem, in both cases, is neoliberalism; it's that which we must fight against. And because the Democratic Party cast Sanders aside for Clinton, who's in the pocket of finance capital, they shot themselves in the foot and left the field to Trump, who thereby won the anti-neoliberal vote. That, no doubt, is right enough, but both premise and conclusion are sadly wrong. The premise is that we have to accept national democracy as the space of political action, and the conclusion, that it's possible to head back to a time before neoliberalism, back to a 'nice capitalism'.

The critique of neoliberalism holds the period before the neoliberal turn up as a positive ideal. But this is to forget the post-war reconstruction of Europe, which American capitalists managed. It's also to forget that Roosevelt's New Deal, before the war, was an explicit attempt to create an alliance between the white working class and capitalist class at the expense of

24

black workers. It was white work and white welfare within the framework of state-sponsored capitalism, and that, of course, is no kind of ideal today. Neither right nor left critiques of neoliberalism are up to much, national welfare is still nationalist and exclusory. It's just not enough, and never has been.[11]

Chapter 2

Politics as Images

Trump's election is the final proof that politics has become image politics; that politics has to do with images; not just in so far as a political message has to take on a particular form or be mediated in a particular medium, but in the sense that politics *is* images. It is not a question of a subsequent wrapping of political content. Politics materializes as images. This process has, of course, been underway for a long time. Walter Benjamin described it in the 1930s and Guy Debord tried to come to terms with it in the 1960s with his analysis of the spectacle. Where Benjamin saw a potential in the emergence of new techniques of reproduction – the emergence of photography, radio and film creating the conditions for visual self-presentation through which modern man could see himself – Debord focused on the forms of subjection the new image machines made possible. Bombardment by images both pacified and isolated. Benjamin and Debord agreed that a shift was taking place that had to do with politics as such. They agreed that politics was becoming something different, due to the explosive growth and variety of reproductive technology and the capacity to produce and circulate images. Modern capitalist society is not only represented and arranged aesthetically but is produced aesthetically. Events materialize as image events with material effects.[12]

We know from the history of art that rulers have always had a need to represent their power. Think of the monarchs of absolutism, the various paintings of the king with all his regalia and symbols of his reign, but also the palaces and castles, the processions and ceremonies. They all testify to the need to create power in an active sense, to show power in all its splendour and effect. It was not just a question of personal vanity. The king's power only existed if it was visible and when it was made present visually or aesthetically. In short, it only existed if everybody could see it. 'This is the world, and I rule. I am God's representative on Earth.' Half godlike, half human. 'The state, that's me.' All such terms and phrases show the performative dimension of power, that power is something that creates, structures, erects, destroys and eternalizes itself in the act. Already the very first state formations were characterized by image politics. The Egyptian Pharaohs and Mesopotamian kings not only built huge palaces and pyramids, they also depicted the very same buildings when they depicted themselves. They were, in other words, very aware of the need to show power and visualize their divine rule.

While power has thus always been 'symbolized' and shown in one way or another, significant changes occurred throughout history. Not least when former religious and political communities were replaced by new ones that considered themselves to be less religious and based on principles of legitimation different from religious ones. This, of course, is the story of secularization and democracy, where democracy constitutes a decisive break with a religious world-image. Today we know better than to argue that we got rid of religion and its furious violence. It is rather the continuity between religion and the ideology of democratic capitalism that is striking. We live in the return of monotheistic violence. In Northern Europe, xenophobic priests rage against foreigners and Muslims above all; in the USA the Christian Right has acquired the post of vice president; in the Middle East militant Islamists ravage; in India a nationalist Hindu president permits anti-Muslim riots and killings. The point is that democracy and nation states foster the same sense of community and undertake many of the same operations that religions used to do: They create meaning and endow individual life with a greater significance. And on the way unleash barbarism and terror. The nation gives shape to a life characterized by volatility and contingency and promises to give it a political infinity or meaning. We are bound together by a common affiliation to something that is bigger than us, something that seems to come from an original past and promise a coming redemption. This, of course, is Benedict Anderson's description of the 'imagined communities of the nation', where national communities respond to the same questions that religions previously answered, but do so in ways that create new communities.

According to Anderson, the introduction of print capitalism was pivotal for the production of the nation's imagined communities. With the book and the newspaper, it became possible to unite brotherhood, power and time in new ways. Thanks to print capitalism, a larger number of people could understand themselves and relate to each other in new ways at the same time across space. Politics has always had an aesthetic dimension, but there's a difference between the techniques with which the political acquires an image dimension. There's a difference between a tomb and a tweet, or a newspaper and a campaign video, or the advanced techniques through which political campaigns appear on Facebook today. This was part of Benjamin's analysis in the essay on the new technologies of reproduction, where he sketched a history from lithography to film, from the self-staging of the monarch to Hitler's inclusion of the mass on film. The history of image politics is to a very large extent a history of the means of representation that kings, the state and politicians have had at their disposal or have been forced into using. Because it is not always easy being subjected to the spectacle, trying to control the image sphere of politics.

It is, of course, Debord, who, more than anyone, has analyzed the image-character of capitalist society and the significance of the emergence of new technologies and media. Following George Lukacs's analysis of Marx's description of the spectacular aspects of capital in the analysis of commodity fetishism, Debord shows how spectacle has become the very essence of late-capitalist society. In the society of the spectacle, life shows itself as an enormous collection of images, where everything lived appears as a representation. Capitalist society is a class society, characterized by fundamental contradictions that can only be solved through a communist revolution, but the spectacle wards off revolution by separating people and uniting them on an image level. New patterns of consumption offer quick identity fixes for the ever-hollower subjects of the spectacular commodity society. The subjects of the society of the spectacle have been worn thin, but an invasion of images, jingles, brands and memes gets them to work and consume without end. Debord talked about this process as a colonization of everyday life, in which human consciousness is taken over by image-like commodities. Benjamin wrote about radio and film; Debord about television. Both of them tried to analyze a process where print capitalism was replaced by a screen capitalism where most people have access to an enormously powerful reproduction apparatus and can produce and circulate photos, videos, diagrams, tweets, hashtags and so on.

Politics has become image politics. Not only because images mediate our existence and we communicate more and more through images, but also because screen media are everywhere. This constitutes a veritable image explosion, where the number of images has grown exponentially, but this also means that politics has changed to such a degree that it is impossible to talk about politics without taking into account the constant flow of images that appears on our screens every day all day long. The image is no longer just a medium but has become politics; in other words, the image is the very material of politics today.

Political sovereignty, then, has always been representational, but before the emergence of spectacle, ordinary people did not have much visual contact with their rulers. It was not until the twentieth century that this changed. New industrial reproduction technologies altered the way politicians behaved. This story is also the story of the coming into being of national democracy, where politicians compete for the electors' votes and support. No medium is better for this than the image that hits the individual voter immediately and excites his or her imagination. And this despite the fact that images are mass produced. A total of 40 million people receive Trump's tweets. Today, politics is a hyper-advanced image regime where power and marketing have fused. We often talk about this in a simplified way as spin, where we tend to think that the spin element appears at the end of the process, as if there's a 'genuine' political message that somehow needs to be served in the right way. As Benjamin and Debord argued, the transformation runs much deeper, politics as such is imaged-based. Very few political decisions are made without spin doctors; before the proposal of any kind of policy, marketing experts have been busy analyzing voting patterns and approval rates. The point being that politicians have to act as if the images are real, as if the images are reality as such.

As a modern phenomenon politics is a process of form-giving. It has to do with giving shape to society and getting the particular shape or form accepted and even better making it appear natural. With Claude Lefort, we can say that politics is the form society gives itself.[13] Politics is about setting up a social space for its subjects, society has to be given a form in the sense of both given a shape and a meaning. For Lefort, this form-giving process has to do with the radical openness of democracy. When the king is decapitated in the democratic revolution the place of power becomes empty. In democracy, no one has privileged access to power. Power is subjected to procedures of periodic redistribution. Democracy is thus characterized by an original indeterminacy. And it is this indeterminacy that Trump is trying hard to annul, referring to himself as somehow beyond the law. He is not a politician, neither really Republican nor Democrat (he used to support the Democrats), he is the boss, a self-made business man that gets things done. He is not involved in any party-political hassles and does not worry about silly juridical commitments or restrictions. Trump will do what it takes to 'Make America Great Again'. And that's it, that's the image he proposes and incarnates.

Following Lefort, we can understand Trump as a sovereign authority, who promises to handle the indeterminacy of democracy, promises to clean up and recreate national community. Trump is completely different to all the traditional politicians, his lack of political experience and limited knowledge of the world outside the USA is not disqualifying in the least, but is in fact testament to Trump's superior candidacy to become president. He suspends politics in the traditional sense. He is from outside and saves the nation. The country is in a deep crisis, everything is falling apart and the political class is incompetent and unable to do anything about the situation. But Trump will remedy all this. He promises to restore America and remove any foreign elements from the national community, curing the sick body:

> Our country is going to hell. Our country is in serious trouble. We don't win anymore. We don't beat China in trade. We don't beat Japan, with their millions and millions of cars coming into this country in trade. We can't beat Mexico, at the border or in trade. We can't do anything right.

But Trump has the strength to reverse this decline. He has the courage to say 'no' and remove the unwanted elements that are threatening the country: Mexicans, Muslims, the politically correct, feminists, blacks, transgender people and so on. Trump is the sovereign who annuls democracy and forces the king's two bodies together again.

The Virtual President

Screen capitalism is the perfect milieu for Trump, who, much more efficiently than Clinton and the various other Republican candidates, was able to put the new social media to use. The tweets of the presidential campaign were genius; Jeb Bush was 'low energy'. It is not necessary to spend millions of dollars on 30-second campaign videos when you can ridicule an opponent with two words on Twitter. Twitter is not a medium for discussion and is therefore ideal for Trump, who is not in the least interested in discussing political issues, but wants to attract attention and cause a stir. Trump had a little more than 3 million followers on Twitter before he announced he would run for president, but he quickly reached 20 million and now has more than 40 million followers. It is not a joke that Trump is the Twitter president. For a politician who wants to win elections, Twitter is a much better medium than TV-commercials or rallies because Twitter lets you communicate directly with your followers on a daily basis without being mediated by news outlets and the press. And when your followers re-tweet your messages you reach even further into the abyss of the electoral mass.

Tweets are the perfect medium for Trump: A tweet has to be short, personal and to the point. There's no space for a worked-out political programme or complex messages but the 140 characters are ample space for Trump's provocations and hallucinatory rants. This is politics as pop culture or pop culture as politics where the distinction between private and public disappears and the political public sphere has finally been reduced to re-tweets. It's not about dialogue; on Twitter it has to be personal and direct. And Trump knows that. He is his own political programme. Strength and success. Trump wants to recreate a nation where the white man makes the calls and where there're no more pointless discussions.

The combination of new media and reality TV gave Trump an advantage. In television, he was already a household name. How many politicians had their own action man? Or a signature catchphrase: 'You're fired!' When *The Apprentice* was at its most popular, more than 20 million viewers followed the weekly show, watching teams competing for Trump's favour. It was about winning and Trump didn't beat around the bush: You either win bigtime or get crushed! That was the lesson of the show. It was this successful businessman – or the pop-cultural staging of one – who ran for president. And Trump behaved and continues to behave as he did in the hire and fire show. He's the same, even if he changes his mind or contradicts himself. That's not important or a problem, it's the Trump character that's important. The successful and rule-breaking white businessman who does what he wants.

That politics today is image politics is something we all know intuitively, but it is also a condition we have great difficulties coming to terms with because it challenges prevailing ideas about politics. Trump is a perfect example of this fact. Political opponents and journalists find it very hard to respond to Trump's quirks and gimmicks because they most often ascribe him a consistency he is precisely lacking. He is a polarity machine who can at the same time thunder against Wall Street and appoint Steven Mnuchin from Goldman Sachs as Secretary of the Treasury, and propose tax reforms benefitting private firms and the wealthiest individuals in the USA. Throughout his campaign and as president, Trump has shown an amazing ability to act chaotically and contradict himself, leaving it very difficult for political opponents and journalists to criticize him. Whenever journalists focus on a specific matter, Trump is busy with new things. He is always two steps ahead. In that way, there is something virtual about Trump. He is able to transform politics into a kind of magic where it is difficult to know what is true or false. Trump contradicts himself, he threatens, he smears and he adopts new positions as he sees fit only to abandon them as quickly as he took them. He is deliberately both swashbuckling and unclear when he makes comments and often prefers tweeting at night, responding to everything from political events to stand-up television shows. But behind all the chaos, there's a project: the project is ultra-nationalist white authoritarianism albeit in a late-capitalist pop-culture version.

As the German cultural critic George Seeßlen writes, Trump suspends the notion of politics as avoiding conflict and acting via consensus with the community – it simply does not make sense what Trump does, it is too strange, and unfit for any elected politician – replacing it with narrations picked up from pop culture.[14] Trump's 'politics' comes from sitcoms, game shows, scripted reality and trash television. The counter-factual, the vulgar, the clownish and the just plain mean might appear misplaced as politics, but it is the very essence of the pop-cultural universe Trump inhabits. Compared to Trump, George W. Bush, who has recently taken up painting, appears something of a Renaissance figure. Trump is the bestseller writer who has never written a single sentence in his financial do it yourself books, the 'architect' of several shiny gold-plated phallus-shaped buildings in cities like New York, Chicago, Miami, Panama City and Istanbul and of course the host of the ultimate hire and fire show on American television.

The forms of demonology

Trump's reality presidency can be regarded as a continuation of what Michael Rogin once called 'Reagan, the Movie', that is Ronald Reagan's visual staging, where he used his actor past as a president.[15] The difference being that with Trump it is not a question of an actor who became a politician but instead there's continuity between mass media representation and politics with Trump as Trump. He is precisely not playing a character, he *is* in character. Trump is Trump. Where Reagan used his roles and disconcertingly seemed to move between two worlds – think of the episode where he mistook his dog for Lassie – Trump is always already in an image space where there's no difference between television series and politics.

This is of course why it does not make sense to appeal to

some kind of Habermasian ideal of communicational rationality when confronted with Trump. The opposition between rational arguments and affect does not work, Trump is precisely suspending such a distinction. The more desperate politicians, experts, journalists and even stand-up comics try to appeal to political reason the more they fail in revealing Trump as a populist demagogue. As Benjamin already stated in the 1930s, modern mass politics cannot be reduced to a question of arguments and enlightened debate. Politics is not some kind of open, rational debate where all are free from economic and political control and everybody strives for the common good. Politics is as much about feelings or pre-individual affects that politicians can mobilize or produce. As Benjamin writes, Hitler and German fascism seek to give the masses expression, something Weimar Republic parliamentary democracy was unable to do. The mass was aesthetically fictionalized by the Nazi party, the mass was transformed into a united visible Aryan community that took part in gigantic visual spectacles watching the Fuhrer and being watched by the Fuhrer. The act of seeing and being seen was the materialization of the Aryan community purified from foreign elements. As members of the party, the mass had a role to play in the racist dramaturgy of National Socialism.

According to Michael Rogin, American politics has always been characterized by what he terms a countersubversive demonology, where the ruling class has produced enemies – from scalping Indians to rebellious black slaves to communist spies to Muslim terrorists – in order to create cohesion and unity, effectively killing the other and producing the People, the American People. The nation is a body that is contaminated by a subversive threat and therefore the individual body and the body politics of the nation has to be protected. A threat to one is a threat to the other and the state has to secure the body on both a micro and macro level, keeping the body healthy and strong. Trump is the culmination of this tradition: The Wall shall stop an ongoing

Mexican invasion that is undermining the national community. The Muslim ban shall prevent Muslim terrorists from entering the country and 3 million migrants have to be thrown out in order to protect the people. The nation is under threat and has to be defended. This is the story the showman stages for an audience eager for racist entertainment.

Chapter 3

A New Fascism

Confronted with Trump, many commentators, academics, intellectuals and activists have asked themselves whether we are experiencing the return of fascism.[16] Does Trump represent American fascism anno 2017? Because fascism is a notoriously difficult term to use, most analyses dismiss the comparison, preferring to characterize Trump as an expression of a variety of right-wing anti-establishment resentment. Trump is not a fascist, the argument goes; he is a populist or a reactionary. There might be something dangerously semi-fascist about many of Trump's statements and his division of the world into the strong and the weak, but the labelling of Trump as a fascist seems far-fetched. Fascism is Hitler, who started the Second World War and orchestrated the industrialized killing of millions of people in extermination camps. Fascism is concentration camps and the SS. Trump wants to build a wall and is determined to introduce a travel ban for Muslims (from certain countries in the Middle East and Asia), but that is not fascism. Trump did hijack the Republican Party, disregarding the party leadership and focusing on his own personal excellence, but he is not talking about building a one-party state. His campaign rallies were characterized not only by violent rhetoric, but also physical assaults, yet his presidency has thus far not involved paramilitary troops marching and parading in the streets – that is, if we disregard the police and the occasional neo-fascist and KKK demonstration. So, the comparison with fascism seems unconvincing.

One of the difficulties involved in comparing anything with fascism is, of course, that the term primarily has a delegitimizing use. To label someone a fascist or, even worse, as resembling Hitler is the same as describing that person as evil or somehow beyond reason. And that's it. Fascism here functions as invective, such as when George W. Bush, Nicolas Sarkozy and Denmark's Minister of Justice, Søren Pape Poulsen, speak of 'Islamofascism' in the context of heightened anti-terror neocolonialism, in which the West invades countries in the Middle East, and militant Islamists respond by engaging in terrorist attacks in Western cities. In such a context, the term fascist only possesses a denigrating function and is used solely as a technique in an ongoing political battle. But fascism can, of course, also be used more analytically, with a view towards analyzing a historical situation and comparing it to previous forms of fascism.

Fascism is, in other words, a difficult term to use and, more often than not, presents an obstacle to analysis rather than serving as a useful category. It is extremely difficult to effectively compare a politician to Hitler. If someone is compared to Hitler, that person is placed beyond the pale, outside respectable politics. This is related, of course, to the non-analysis of Hitler and Nazism. Hitler and Nazism have become floating signifiers in Western pop culture, with Nazism reduced to black leather boots, aggressive salutes and dead bodies. The pop-cultural representation of Nazism has tended to transform fascism into something both recognizable and kitschy, both disgusting and sexy, all the while upholding it as a phenomenon with a unique place in history as the epitome of barbaric excess, as something that we need not analyze but can simply reject. There is something pathological about fascism, which makes it difficult to identify its political and economic conditions of possibility: Those were different times, the Nazis were just evil, we are different today, the 1930s are so long ago, and so on.

Calling someone a fascist means scolding someone. It is rarely part of political or economic analysis. In 1951, the conservative philosopher Leo Strauss described how comparing a political statement with something Hitler said was the same as invalidating it. You are a vegetarian, Hitler was a vegetarian, ergo you are a Nazi. Strauss called this *reduction ad Hitlerum*. We find a similar process in the so-called Godwin's Law, according to which any discussion on the internet ends with someone being compared to Hitler – the point being that a comparison with Hitler, or 'playing the Hitler card', is just a way of delegitimizing one's opponents.

The conclusion seems to be that fascism is absent from contemporary political analysis, becoming a kind of ahistorical ultimate evil. This does not, however, mean that fascism has disappeared as a political phenomenon. It is difficult to avoid kneejerk reactions when contemporary phenomena are described as fascist, but this does not mean that certain phenomena should *not* be labelled as fascist if that is what they are. It just means that we need to be precise in our use of the term.

It is, in other words, important to define the way in which the term fascism is being used. The starting point for any discussion of contemporary fascism must be the interwar European fascist movements, for which there exists a comprehensive literature. Such a discussion, however, ought to be capable of using the term outside this specific historical context as well. If we can speak of socialism, anarchism, conservatism and liberalism as both historical phenomena and contemporary ideologies that change over time, then we can also speak of fascism as an ideology that transforms across history. It would be wrong to assume that fascism is a unique political phenomenon that appears in the early decades of the twentieth century and then completely disappears following the Second World War. Reducing fascism to evil incarnate is simply an ideological manoeuvre that serves to uphold an existing social order that to some extent legitimizes itself as a continuation of the struggle against fascism. Fascism is, unfortunately, not something that can be limited to the period between the first and second world wars, and, confronted with phenomena such as Donald Trump in the USA, Front National in France, Golden Dawn in Greece, Orban's Fidesz Party in

Hungary, UKIP in Great Britain and the Danish People's Party in Denmark, it is important to make historical comparisons. If one engages in a reading of Trump's inauguration speech, as I shall do in the next chapter, it becomes evident that a discussion about fascism is precisely what is needed. There is an explicit ultra-nationalist dimension to Trump's discourse, which speaks of recreating an original American community that is currently under threat. Trump is the strong leader who will exclude un-American elements and unite the American people.

As Ian Kershaw has shown, fascism cannot be reduced to the story of one individual; Hitler alone cannot explain German fascism.[17] The strong leader who transcends ordinary politics does, however, play an important role in fascist ideology. The strong leader embodies the nation. In terms of political affect, the leader *is* the nation. There is no distinction between the two, and the leader transforms the people into a family, of which he is the father who must protect and care for the household. Fascism contains ideas of 'natural hierarchy' and 'natural order', an order that the leader recreates and of which the leader is in charge. With the fascist leader, the invisible violence of the household becomes a political programme. This is one explanation for Trump's misogyny and racism, for Trump's outright contempt for women and non-white people. On the basis of reverse victimization, Trump presents himself as a new-old, 'natural' order.

There are, of course, important differences between Trump and the interwar fascist leaders, differences conditioned by their historical settings, but Trump appeals to and utilizes many of the same emotions that were mobilized by Mussolini and Hitler, and he deploys a discourse promising national rebirth through exclusion of the other, carried out by a strong leader. The targets of exclusion differ, as do the ways in which such exclusion is meant to be accomplished. For Hitler, it was primarily the Jews who represented a secret connection between communism and finance capital, while Trump targets all non-white Americans (especially Mexicans and Latinos) and Muslims. African Americans represent a threat to Trump's vision of a genuine American community and thus need to be controlled and kept at bay by the police.

Trump's fascism is very different from that of interwar Europe, but this should not come as a surprise, given that fascism has always appealed to national specificities and presented itself as an authentic expression of national characteristics. Italian Fascism, Hitler's Nazism and Franco's Falangism in Spain did so, as did French, Greek and Romanian fascists. Fascism is characterized precisely by the ability to channel a nation's imagined 'natural' qualities. As Robert O. Paxton writes, fascism is in this sense always local, and it would be a mistake to believe that it only takes the form of brown shirts with shoulder straps and book burnings in the streets.[18] As Paxton writes in 2004, long before Trump became president, the symbols of contemporary American fascism would probably not resemble the European 'original'. The swastika will be replaced with stars and stripes because fascism will always use recognizable symbolism. The fasces of Italian Fascism were not exotic and strange in 1920s Italy, and Nazism's mixture of antisemitism and antisocialism belonged to the *Zeitgeist* of 1930s Germany. These were symbols that were already known to the masses, just like Trump's baseball cap and macho locker-room talk of today. They are meant to confirm and create identity. The 'Make America Great Again' caps produce a community, not unlike the team jersey in American football or basketball, dividing friends from foes. At first glimpse, these do not appear especially fascist, but they are nonetheless litmus tests for recognizing both the national community and the enemy within.

The contradictions of fascism

One of the challenges involved in determining something as fascist is that fascism is a contradictory ideology that promises resurrection of a former or 'original' greatness but does so through the newest and most modern technologies of communication and means of production. This was one of the points in Benjamin's diagnosis of fascism as an 'aestheticizing of politics'. Italian and German fascism used new reproduction technologies to stage a spectacle in which the masses could find expression while cheering the leader.[19] We see a similar process with Trump, who also combines the appeal to a strong White America with an effective use of new social media. By spouting daily Twitter messages and ranting lies concerning topics ranging from non-existent terrorist attacks ('last night in Sweden') to climate change as a conspiracy of the Chinese Communist Party, Trump is able to dominate the screens. He is a master of image politics. He is always on and capable of communicating directly to the people through Twitter. This represents a late-capitalist realization of the French fascist Robert Brasillach's dream of being everywhere (*Je suis partout*). This omnipresence grants Trump a sense of intimacy. He is the returned father, who is not mediated by media and journalists but instead speaks directly to members of the family. There is an unbreakable and unmediated relationship between Trump – the leader – and the masses. There is no distance; Trump is always there. Like popstars today, Trump is constantly appearing across an extended network of liquid screens.

Most political theorists agree that fascism is ideologically unstable. In the words of Alice Yager Kaplan, fascism is a polarity machine that unites opposites, such as modern and anti-modern, construction and destruction, abstract and literal, popular and top-down.[20] In contrast with what many might expect, the interwar fascist movements were composite and less ideologically consistent than they appear in retrospect. There is nevertheless a set of features that unites the various fascisms, features that make it possible to speak of fascism today even though the political phenomena we analyze do not describe themselves as fascist. Mussolini, Hitler and Franco defined themselves as fascists. Very few politicians do so today. In the wake of the Holo-caust and the Second World War, the historical weight of fascism is overwhelming. But fascism cannot be reduced to a previous era's symbolic form and specific xenophobias. That Trump does not appear in uniform and does not rail against a Jewish con-spiracy should not exempt him from the label of fascist. Fascism is not an invariable ideology but is, like all ideologies, in con-stant movement, shaping itself after the present. So, of course, fascism is different today than it was in the 1930s. If Mussoli-ni and Hitler spearheaded fascist movements that fought in the streets against revolutionary and reformist socialists, Trump is the natural outcome of an expanded entertainment industry, a star who transforms racism and misogyny into light entertain-ment and one-liners. With Trump, fascism has gone from being a pop-cultural theme – a subject of films, TV series and memorials – to being a political project in itself. Today's cultural industrial production apparatus produces nationalist myth as ready-made affect politics.

Enzo Traverso, a scholar of Italian totalitarianism, recently described Trump as part of a wider post-fascist wave that in-cludes phenomena such as Brexit and the rise of different far-right parties in Europe like Front National in France.[21] Post-fas-cism explicitly distances itself from historical interwar fascism but nonetheless constructs a fascist narrative of a strong leader who must protect the ethnonational community, recreating an imagined glorious past. Fascism is the idea of an original com-munity exposed to external threats that must somehow be re-moved. This is the task of the strong leader. According to Tra-verso, this is the core of the stories Trump and Marine Le Pen tell about themselves and the ethnonational community they seek to protect. But unlike the interwar fascist movements, nation-al rebirth is no longer conceived as a suspension of the nation-al parliamentary system. Traverso therefore proposes the term post-fascism. Post-fascism differs from interwar European fascism but also from the various neo-fascist groups that have arisen after the Second World War because post-fascism is less about extra-parliamentary movements than about parties and politicians fighting for votes within established political systems, all the while challenging these systems or augmenting their inherent nationalist and exclusionary dimensions. Post-fascism is thus fascism's attempt to dress up as a respectable political alternative that is at once on the inside and on the outside.

Front National in France is a good example of this development. The party has gone from being a subversive anti-party connected to French Vichy fascism and the French anti-decolonization movement to becoming a credible alternative within the established political system, with the party's leader reaching the second round of the French presidential election in the spring of 2017. Post-fascist parties all denounce local and global political elites. The old political parties are not protecting the people and have allowed multinational companies to move jobs abroad and – even worse – do nothing to prevent migrants from entering the country, even though they are intent on destroying the nation. But post-fascism presents itself as more of a continuation, unlike the explicit break sought by interwar fascism. Le Pen is protecting the Republic, not destroying it. This is the partial transformation that drives Traverso to use the term post-fascism; fascism is shedding its revolutionary suit. Though Traverso does not make this explicit, the point is that because it is so difficult to imagine a non-capitalist world today, fascism need not present itself as revolutionary. There is no coherent revolutionary international communist movement as there was from 1917 to 1937. There is thus no direct threat that fascism must counter (and imitate). In the vocabulary of this book, we could say that fascism has a *preventive*, counter-revolutionary function; it is preventing the coming into being of a revolutionary perspective.

I am uncertain about Traverso's argument that post-fascism is not anti-systemic in the same manner as interwar fascism. Fas-

cism is never truly anti-systemic. Fascism is always capital pre-
serving, its 'revolutionary' project is always carried out with a
view to securing the accumulation of capital. Traverso's distinction between fascism and post-fascism risks introducing a difference that is perhaps less important than the continuity between
interwar fascism and the late-capitalist fascism of Trump and Le
Pen. In terms of ideology and political economy, fascism remains
grounded in racist exclusion and some kind of state capitalism
in which the law of value is controlled though government economic policy. Trump's xenophobic presidential decrees and the
white washing of neo-fascist murder after Charlottesville is fascism anno 2017, fascism that cannot say its name out loud and
appears in a superficial pop-cultural form that differs from the
grandiose proclamations of the interwar years, in which Nazism
presented itself as a Thousand Year Reich. Trump's dream world
is an imaginary 1950s, not some World Reich of the middle age.
He remains within the world of pop-cultural fiction and is interested in recreating a fictionalized 1952 America. But it is nonetheless fascism if we define fascism as a violent political project
centred on the notion of a threatened ethno-nationalist community protected by a strong leader who is capable of preventing
the coming into being of a real challenge to the established political order and capitalist mode of production.

This does not mean that the 'old' fascism and Trump's
late-capitalist version are the same. Trump's late-capitalist fascism is more banal than those of the interwar years in Europe,
is somehow a 'cheaper' version, in which references to national destiny and an identification between Germany and Ancient
Greece or between Mussolini and Caesar have been replaced by
vulgar ideas of power, success and money. Trump is not sovereign. There is little heterogeneity in the sense of Georges Bataille
in Trump's fascist project.[22] He is not a descending God in the
manner of Riefenstahl's filmic representation of Hitler. Trump is
gold-plated buildings and golf clubs, young wives and bizarre

rants. If fascism once mimicked religion and high art, it is now pop culture incarnate. This explains the element of pure surface in Trump. Fascism has always been characterized by a strange lack of historical depth, combining contradictory ideologies and elements, but Trump takes this to new heights. This explains the strange shallowness when Trump speaks and employs an ultra-nationalist vocabulary. It comes off as artificial, it is as if Trump plays honest when he babbles and tweets. The numerous executive orders are right out of a fascist copybook but nonetheless appear more simulacrum than real policy. He is a fascist but a postmodern kind of fascist. His fascism is a pastiche, an entertainment-industrial fascism, in which all acts and statements are in quotes. This is a kind of 'fascism light' that is ignorant of its own history and truly believes in its slogans. But such a fascism can turn out just as violent as the 'original' version, of course.

If fascism was formerly characterized by antisemitism, the new post-fascism is primarily Islamophobic. Trump and Le Pen are both rabid Islamophobes, effectively using the threat of militant Islamic terrorism by blowing it out of all proportion, transforming it into an outright Islamophobia that affects all Africans and Arabs in the West, including non-practising Muslims, Sikhs and groups of African Christians. In the Islamophobic discourse, Islam takes on the shape of a conspiracy: Islam is not just a religion but is also a characteristic of that portion of the population that needs to be excluded. It is the enemy within, which is in cahoots with enemies abroad that seek to destroy the national community. The politics of fear knows no limits and people who flee from war or migrate to get a better life become enemies, a threat to our identity. Trump's attempts to impose a travel ban on travellers from seven Muslim countries says it all. The national community must be protected.

Chapter 4

'America'

Let us take a closer look at the story Trump tells. I will focus on Trump's inauguration speech of 20 January 2017. The speech was a textbook example of fascist rhetoric. In the speech, Trump used three classic fascist tropes: He spoke of the people as a threatened national community, he spoke of himself as a strong leader ready to shake up a corrupt political elite and set things straight, and he proclaimed a national rebirth through the exclusion of non-Americans. The starting point for Trump's narration is decline. Using short sentences, Trump narrates a story of America's destruction, describes how the country has been turned into a battlefield on which the local political elite has permitted foreign companies to steal American jobs, effectively hollowing out American society. Trump wants to stop this development and restore America. He wants to give power back to the people and recreate American greatness. As he puts it, Americans are faced with a huge task: 'We, the citizens of America, are now joined in a great national effort to rebuild our country and to restore its promise to all of our people.' The American people has lost its orientation and been broken down. A political elite has allowed foreign powers to run amok, destroying the country's industry and infrastructure. 'For a long time, a small group in our nation's Capital has reaped the rewards of government while the people have borne the cost. Washington flourished – but the people did not share in its wealth.' Washington betrayed the people. The people have been demeaned by the political elite, who do not care about those people it is meant to represent.

> The establishment protected itself, but not the citizens of our country. Their victories have not been your victories; their

triumphs have not been your triumphs; and while they celebrated in our nation's Capital, there was little to celebrate for struggling families across our land. That all changes – starting right here, and right now.

Trump's election is an end to this development, an end to decline and betrayal. Trump's presidency marks a new beginning, a break from the past. Things have to change. The people will once again take centre stage, with Trump as leader.

Today's ceremony...has very special meaning. Because today we are not merely transferring power from one Administration to another, or from one party to another – we are transferring power from Washington, DC and giving it back to you, the American people...January 20th 2017, will be remembered as the day the people became the rulers of this country again...

Trump is on a mission to restore American greatness. He is drawing a line in the sand; the rout ends here. The American people will come back stronger than ever or are perhaps already great again thanks to Trump's electoral victory. 'From this moment on, it's going to be America First.'

Whereas most of Trump's speeches are cacophonic, often delirious rants with numerous grammatical errors, the speech on Capitol Hill was relatively coherent and almost classical in style and structure, and Trump had a script to which he stuck throughout the speech. The TV star and businessman, the anti-establishment candidate, now addressed the nation as president. Trump started out by thanking Obama but, in accordance with his campaign, the presidential and reconciliatory tone was quickly replaced by a dramatic story of national loss and a coming recovery. This was a story about villains, enemies and an 'America' – the national community – that had been neglected but was going to get better and stronger, stronger than ever before. It was a leader who spoke to his people. The presidential and statesmanlike were replaced by an exclusionary discourse in which the captain rallied his troops. It was the leader of the people who spoke of threats from enemies who had prospered from the ruination of the American community, and it was the leader who promised redemption. Trump quickly moved from the statesmanlike to the role of the strong leader, though he refrained from the direct personal attacks that had characterized his campaign and have characterized his subsequent behaviour.

The people and the national community

Trump narrated a dramatized history of an endangered community's decline. The notion of 'the people' was central to the narration. Throughout the speech, Trump speaks of the people and the nation as a spiritual community that is distinct from the state and even from the population that is normally seen as constituting the country. It was 'America' and not the United States of America Trump talked about. He did not say 'Make USA great again' but 'Make America great again'. 'America' being a kind of mystical figure that does not include all the people that are in the USA, but includes something different, both more and less than the actual persons in the country. This is not just because of the existence of a whole mass of people (such as illegal immigrants) who do not belong to Trump's American community but also because of the existence of America's indigenous population, African Americans and all the groups Trump has mocked and ridiculed during and since the campaign. Trump is expressly *not* talking about the diversity of the country, its cultural and religious differences. He speaks of 'the people' as a united subject, the people as one. It is in this sense that 'America' includes more than just the actual bodies in the USA. Trump is constructing a symbolic and spiritual community, one that transcends the actual individuals present in the country at this moment. This is a mystical national community that is connected to, but also distinct from, the United States of America as a state, as a geographical and territorial entity, and from the mass of people who live there today. 'America' is more than the USA. The USA is just a state, while 'America' is a spiritual entity, a mission, a destiny. This is something that Washington and the political elite do not understand. But Trump is taking over and rebuilding America, making America great again.

The idea of an original America is central to Trump's speech. This is an America that is more than the state and its institutions, even more than the country's population. It is America as an authentic group of people, or perhaps an American tribe, that Trump wishes to gather again and make strong. 'From this day forward, a new vision will govern our country. From this moment on, it's going to be America First.' America is an identity, not a set of rules or a constitution. It is precisely not Washington or all the different parts of the state administration, the two chambers of Congress, the presidency or the courts. It is a mythological entity that one cannot reject but that transforms politics into a question of transindividual affects. It is politics as mass politics, in which the individual not only casts a vote but becomes part of something much bigger, becomes part of a political-religious community. 'We are one nation – and their pain is our pain.' America is a political body that Trump will care for. 'We share one heart, one home, and one glorious destiny.'

'America First' is a quote. It was the motto and name of a political movement in the early 1940s, the America First Committee. The movement gathered together stern opponents of American participation in the Second World War. Headed by businesspeople such as the newspaper mogul and virulent anti-communist Randolph Hearst and the fascist car manufacturer Henry Ford, the movement agitated in favour of American isolationism on the basis of an idea of the supremacy of the white man. Leading members of this group, such as the pilot Charles Lindbergh, not only expressed sympathy for Nazi Germany but spoke of the necessity of the white race engaging in a fight for self-preservation. Jews and blacks had a negative influence on the white race. Trump is the re-actualization of this American fascism. In his campaign and as president, Trump has used hidden historical quotes, digging into the history of American fascism and referring to outright fascist movements in American history. 'America First' is one example. Trump also, of course, refers to a tradition of white supremacy. In his inauguration speech, he refers to 'the silent majority', a notion Richard Nixon deployed in the late 1960s to designate the white population in the USA who were opposed to the civil rights movement, opposed to the partial dismantling of the state-sanctioned privileging of whites and the new experimental lifestyles that surfaced in the counter-cultures of the time.

In the speech, Trump effectively gestures towards a number of reactionary historical movements in the USA that have defended the supremacy of the white race and sought to prevent any end to state-sanctioned racism, which was a reality from 1605 until 1965. Trump plays on the racism and nationalism that has survived many places in the USA and that has historically been expressed by politicians such as Andrew Jackson, George Wallace, Ronald Reagan and Pat Buchanan. These are politicians who evoked a Manichean worldview in which it is necessary to protect the people from external threats such as Indians, socialists and the politically correct. Trump is a master in this political fearmongering and gives it a whole new dimension when he, in his inauguration speech, talks about how the country has been subjected to 'carnage'.

His speech also contains the phrase 'forgotten men and women of our country', who 'will be forgotten no longer'. Franklin D. Roosevelt spoke of forgotten men in a radio speech during the 1932 presidential election, when he discussed the need to include the 'forgotten, the unorganized but the indispensable' men from the USA's working class in the USA's economy. It was necessary to include 'the forgotten man at the bottom of the economic pyramid' in order to get out of the economic crisis, Roosevelt argued. The industrial worker and the farmer were forgotten, but they constituted the backbone of a new American society. The New Deal was the programme meant to make visible and include the forgotten men, transforming them into Fordist workers and Keynesian consumers. Modern society was to be built by the forgotten men. This development was a cornerstone in the coming into being of post-war welfare society, with minimum wages and social rights. Workers became legitimate citizens in the USA, with money in their pockets, and many even received access to education. Roosevelt's project and the New Deal's success was, however, based on the exclusion of African Americans who remained largely not just forgotten but also invisible, not to mention subjected to racism and discrimination. The New Deal was in this regard a continuation of an established discourse on 'the forgotten men' in America, in which 'the forgotten men' are the white working class. They have been neglected and must be included. Already in 1883, the social-Darwinist sociologist William Graham Sumner had spoken of 'the forgotten men' who were being corrupted by poor and weak people who were destroying the country. According to Sumner, setting up a social safety net for the poor would be an enormous mistake, and it was much better to let the market dominate. The white bourgeoisie could not and should not help white workers; individual workers had to take care of themselves and rise out of poverty, thereby confirming their superiority as white men. The white worker should show his worth by working his way out of poverty. Roosevelt's New Deal represented a break with the laissez faire economy proposed by Sumner, but it was nevertheless a continuation of a racist policy that divided the population into whites and everyone else. The notion of the forgotten men who must be included was historically a lever for a class alliance between the white capitalist class and the white working class. The latter distanced itself from the non-white working class in the USA, receiving political rights and bigger pay cheques as a result. By allying itself with the white upper class, the white workers secured privileges and ensured that they would never fall to the bottom of the social ladder, fall as low as the black workers. The white worker was never just a poor proletarian but was always also a white citizen and thereby privileged. This is the way racism and sexism work: They are systems for distributing material advantages to the benefit of the white man. Instead of joining the freed slaves and other coloured poor, the white working class joined forces with the white upper class, thereby effectively derailing the USA's revolutionary potential. This is the story, told by WEB Du Bois and others, of how white workers defended their own position at the expense of other parts of the working class by allying with the local capitalist class.[23]

Trump uses a racist and nationalist mythology about the forgotten men who need vindication. Trump re-actualizes Sumner and Roosevelt's narrative of the white working class. This is the group he is addressing. It is the white worker who has lost his job because the government has allowed companies to move production to China. There is an explicit social Darwinian dimension to Trump's description of the strong and united people, the decline, the threats and the need for exclusion and unity. There is a natural hierarchy, and Trump is the one who will succeed in re-establishing it.

Trump's language is structured around the opposition between 'winners' and 'losers', 'us' and 'them', 'order' and 'chaos'. These oppositions appear in his attacks on other politicians and the media, 'it's me against them', and when he speaks about the country and the world, about America against the rest of the world, including everything from NATO and allies like the EU to Mexico, China and North Korea. Trump and America are winners and all the rest are losers. They are weak, and Trump is the leader precisely because he is strong. There is a circularity here: I am a winner because I am strong, and I am strong because I am winning. The opposition between winners and losers is a latter-day version of the old 'survival of the fittest' logic. Politics is a question of strength and about cheating others. It is a question of racial and ethnonational communities and oppositions. The project is a revitalization of an exclusionary capitalist order defined by racial religious features: 'America'. This America has been devastated by the concerted actions of local elites and foreign powers, including international institutions, countries like Mexico and China and religions like Islam. They have colluded and brought destruction to the great American nation. This is the development Trump has devoted himself to opposing. He is uniting the American people, making America great again.

The 'America' Trump keeps addressing and gesturing towards is a mystical national community. It is not the United States of America; it is much more. 'America' functions like the French syndicalist Georges Sorel's idea of a social myth.[24] According to Sorel, strong political ideas are important because the modern world is characterized by a lack of energy and vitalism. Ideas like resurrection and revolution can mobilize the masses by virtue of their mystical power. Beyond the occasional casting of votes – which only mobilizes the masses briefly, if at all – social myths inspire and involve the masses in a much more inclusive way than do ordinary politics, which are characterized by limited participation. Myth transforms politics into mass politics and suspends ordinary ideas of political reasoning. Myth cannot be dismissed, for it is neither right nor wrong, and is not realizable in any straightforward way but instead points towards a much more radical political change. The shift from USA to America is one such change. As Trump says in the inauguration speech, 'We are transferring power from Washington, DC and giving it back to you, the American People.' Friday, 20 January 2017 was thus not just the swearing in of a new president; it was something much more. It was the creation of a new system. By electing Trump, the people have elected themselves.

The mythological America Trump evokes has striking parallels with the imagined communities of European fascism. Both Italian fascism and German Nazism were characterized by the idea of the unity of the nation, and the task of the fascist parties was to recreate a glorious, imagined national past ruled by Italy and the Aryan race, with the national and racial community remaining intact. The nation had been threatened by external threats, which needed to be made visible and eliminated. Parliamentary chaos, economic crisis and experimental lifestyles endangered the nation. The incipient threat of a communist revolution was constantly evoked. For German Nazism, the idea of the Jews' culture-destroying nature was, of course, central. But whatever the differences, the national community was under threat and had to be protected. Threatening foreigners needed to be removed and national unity secured at all costs.

We find fascism's myth of the nation, the original national community, in Trump's idea of 'America', just as the idea of Italy and the Aryan race constitutes a higher ethical reality. The nation must pursue their collective destiny. The political programme seeks to produce a new spiritual community or recover a lost original community that has been destroyed by politicians, Mexicans, Muslims, Feminists and so on. The nation is a sublime ethical order that, in an active sense, must be produced. Indeed, it must be produced as a defensive operation in which the national community entrenches itself.

Trump is not Hitler. Nor is he Mussolini. There are, however, parallels in the ways in which both Trump and the two fascist leaders discuss the national community. The people represent an imaginary ethical community that emerges from the nation. The American people of whom Trump speaks is a united people, and Trump's mission is to unite a divided people. Divided by political disagreement and exploited by politicians and Wall

Street, the people have been broken. Trump speaks of 'an American carnage'. This carnage must come to an end. The national community must rise up again. 'We must protect our borders from the ravages of other countries making our products, stealing our companies, and destroying our jobs. Protection will lead to great prosperity and strength.' Trump describes America as a body that needs protection from external threats. The weak and the sick need to go. During his campaign, Trump went so far as to ridicule the handicapped, including mocking a handicapped journalist from the *New York Times*. Everything foreign and weak must be removed. We will get rid of all the immigrants, impose a ban on Muslims entering the country, put the blacks in prison and build a huge wall along the border with Mexico.

The government is to blame for the nation's disarray. Washington has allowed foreign powers to enter America and undermine its economy. 'The government has bled our country dry,' Trump said during the campaign. In his inauguration speech, he continued this attack on Washington, castigating the government. As president, Trump has continued to engage in fierce attacks on a seemingly endless stream of enemies. He has lunged out at the media, his own political party, the Democrats, the FBI, the CIA and a long list of government agencies as well as numerous foreign countries, including many former allies. During the campaign, he often criticized Wall Street – 'they are getting away with murder' – but has more or less ceased this criticism since taking office. He vowed to break up the big banks and force 'the finance guys' to pay higher taxes, yet his tune changed dramatically after the election. Trump immediately stacked his cabinet with Wall Street players, rolled back banking regulations and ended 2017 by proposing a huge tax reform that benefits the banks and the 1 per cent. This change of heart reminds one of Hitler's attacks on German capital before taking power. German companies were responsible for Germany's downfall, Hitler said. This did not prevent him from receiving huge donations and support from leading factions of the German capitalist class (notably the Keppler Circle). We find the same duality in Trump, for whom the contradictions are even greater, given that Trump is himself a businessman and owner of a multinational franchise empire, with offshoots in many countries. Trump's programme was to 'drain the swamp' of bureaucracy and lobbyists in Washington. Like Hitler, Trump thunders against global capitalism and a weak political elite – 'politicians prospered – but the jobs left, and the factories closed' – all the while handing out huge tax cuts to the banks and his millionaire friends.

The American body must be cured. Trump, the wealthy businessman and successful reality TV star, is the doctor who cures the patient by uniting it and eliminating foreign threats: the racially oppressed, immigrants, women and LBGTQ individuals. 'You're fired!' as Trump said in his catchphrase conclusion to the 189 episodes of *The Apprentice*. Washington, feminists, Mexicans, black criminals: they all have to go. And the people rally behind Trump. His political vision is this united, whole people. America First. America for Americans. A community animated by the dream of self-sufficiency and greatness. Greatness as purity. 'When America is united, America is totally unstoppable' Trump chants, equating unity with strength. It is necessary to tighten the borders, build walls. Only by fortifying the community can America become great once more. Instead of international trade agreements, America must pull back and focus on the domestic market, stimulated by the state. 'We will follow two simple rules: buy American and hire American.' This is the recipe for Trump's late-capitalist fascist solution, in which the state places tariffs on foreign goods, supports local industry, creates demand and provides docile workers to a local capitalist class that has lost out on globalization.

Trump's focus on a united people carries specific connotations. As noted above, it is the white middle class that constitutes the model and that is meant to inhabit the 'America' that

Trump wishes to create or recreate. 'The wealth of our middle class has been ripped from their homes and then redistributed across the entire world.' It is the white middle class that Trump is addressing. This was the case during the campaign and in his inauguration speech. Trump talks about the problems of the middle class as though they were universal, as though they were everyone's problems. 'Americans want great schools for their children, safe neighbourhoods for their families, and good jobs for themselves.' The mystical 'America' narrated by Trump is the America of the white middle class. This is Trump's ideal. It is an America with good schools, safe neighbourhoods and good jobs. But hypostasizing the middle class and its dreams is itself exclusionary: everybody who does not identify with this dream is not part of Trump's America. They are enemies of 'America'. In his inauguration speech, Trump speaks primarily of foreign threats, foreign powers and other countries. During the campaign, he talked about immigrants, both legal and illegal, and he also virulently attacked the racially oppressed, Muslims and other 'non-Americans', including feminists, LBGTQ individuals and the politically correct. Trump divides the population into two: on the one hand those who belong to his American middle-class society, to Trump's imaginary 'America', and on the other are those who do not conform to this image of the white middle class but instead threaten it.

The Italian philosopher Giorgio Agamben has described the operation that occurs in Trump's way of talking about the American people, in which a certain class or section of the population represent the united and complete people ('America'), and those who do not fit into this American Dream are excluded. Agamben's approach is etymological, and he explains that the notion of 'people' is characterized by an originary split that makes it necessary to continually remove the lower classes, who Agamben calls people with a lowercase 'p'. 'People' designates both the people as a whole, the people as an undivided political corpus, Trump's 'America' *and* the subdivision of people with a lowercase 'p', all the excluded and suffering, the migrants and the inmates. As Agamben puts it, 'the same term names the constitutive political subject as well as the class that is excluded – de facto, if not de jure – from politics.'[25] The people is at once 'the whole of the citizenry as a unitary body politics,' 'the total state of the sovereign and integrated citizens' and is 'the banishment – either court of miracles or camp – of the wretched, the oppressed, and the vanished'.[26] Trump is determined to produce a people in the first sense, a 'People' with an uppercase 'p', the constitutive political subject, the imagined originary community that has decomposed or been destroyed but may now be recreated or re-emerge. It is about giving form to the people, about the people giving itself a clear and determinate form. 'When America is united, America is totally unstoppable.' The people should constitute itself as sovereign, become itself as an autonomous and self-reliant power, yet the people with a lowercase 'p' continue to haunt the People: naked life, blacks, migrants keep appearing. This split always surfaces, making it necessary to build a wall, to ban people, perhaps to torture and kill them. The miserable and the foreign must be removed. America can only become great again if it rids itself of the people with a lowercase 'p'. The nation has to be protected, and the solution is to exclude anything and everything un-American, whether in terms of trade, culture or foreign policy. By locking itself behind the nation's borders, America can reaffirm its greatness. 'A new national pride will stir our souls, lift our sights, and heal our divisions.'

Trump wants to get rid of everything un-American. That is the project. 'America' must be made totally present; there can be no dark spots. As Trump puts it: 'At the bedrock of our politics will be a total allegiance to America', the nation above everything else, 'America First'. The national community is the foundation and the goal. America produces itself in a kind of auto-erotic process in which the dialectical oscillation between the

People with an uppercase 'p' and the people with a lowercase 'p' is eliminated, and the People come out the victors. 'America will start winning again, winning like never before.'

The fascist leader

America is going to win again. Trump will take care of that. His election represents a turning point. 'This American carnage stops right here and stops right now.' 20 January 2017 is the beginning of something new. It is the return of the real nation, the coming into itself of the authentic community. Thanks to Trump and his election, 'America' will be great again. Trump presents himself as the only solution to the carnage. Only Trump can ensure recovery and care for the nation. He is the saviour. He can recreate America's superiority. His election is a promise, a promise of the recreation of American hegemony.

There is a peculiar temporality to Trump's inauguration speech. Trump is simultaneously the solution and the announcement of a coming solution. His candidacy, the election and the inauguration constitute a turning point or indicate that something is about to change. Trump is the solution and the promise of a solution. 'I'll do it', he says, or, 'we'll do it together'. Now or very soon. The point is that Trump is different, different from Washington. The rot has stopped or will stop soon. America will become great again. Obama, Mexicans, the politicians, the feminists, Clinton, China, black criminals and so on have destroyed America. But it stops here. 'From this day forward, a new vision will govern our land.' Trump keeps repeating that he is the one who can stop the decline. He is the one who is capable of getting the USA out of the crisis and transforming it into 'America'.

Trump is the best. That was in many ways the essence of Trump's campaign, and that continues to be his political programme as president. Bragging and excessive self-promotion replace any kind of traditional political programme. Trump is president because he is rich and successful. He keeps boasting about his fortune, his buildings and his global business empire. He is extremely intelligent, a genius in fact, 'a very stable genius'. Everybody loves him, especially women. Women love him. Of course they do. He is strong and supremely wealthy.

The emphasis on the strong leader who is not part of the political system is the second fascist feature in Trump's inauguration speech. Trump presents himself as a kind of superhuman who can halt the American carnage and recreate America, making America great again. He is the superhero who comes from outside and solves all the problems that ordinary politicians are incapable of solving.

The belief that Trump is different is central to the 'Make America great again' discourse. It is of course important that Trump ran for president as Republican, but he was not part of the party's usual repertoire, and was formerly a Democrat. Trump transcends party politics and is, first and foremost, American. He is against the system, he took over the Republican Party, and resistance from the party elite confirms his outsider status. The continual resistance to Trump and all his crazy statements endow him with authenticity: he is the real deal, unentangled in party politics and free of the stench of Washington. It is therefore Trump who can turn the tide. 'Ordinary' politics is part of the problem. We need something different, something new. We need a real leader who is not afraid to do things differently and act radically, meaning remove the problems at the root. Trump is the tough guy who can say 'no' to IS, to China and to Mexico, but also to the UN and NATO. He will take no heed of the petitions of black criminals and politically correct students who want to remove 'beautiful' Civil War statues. Trump can say no and hit back. America has become weak, but Trump will restore American strength, turn chaos and carnage into greatness.

Trump is a different leader from Mussolini and Hitler. They were militaristic whereas he is not. The swastika has been replaced by a baseball cap and a very long red tie. Disciplined troops marching through the streets or standing in long lines in front of the leader have been replaced by a cheering, beer-drinking crowd dressed in polo shirts and T-shirts. The party insignia has been replaced by fan cultural emblems that have more to do with American football and pop music than with the military. Trump's baseball cap proves that he is one of the people, just like you and me – only more successful. Together with Trump, we can all be unbelievably successful. Yet the emphasis on the need for a strong leader is the same. America needs a strong leader who can end the misery and heal the national community. Trump is the heroic warrior who removes the corrupt politicians and hands power back to the people.

If Mussolini and Hitler were leaders of political movements, then Trump is the reality TV star and businessman who is completely independent and accountable to no one, unconstrained by any political programme. Trump can thus say whatever he feels like. And this he does, including tweeting against 'out of control media', attacking FBI officials and depicting Hillary Clinton getting hit in the back with a golf ball. The fight against the administration and the civil service and against the news media is a direct continuation of Trump's daily rants on Twitter against everybody and everything. Not a single day has gone by when Trump has not attacked named politicians, journalists, NFL players and celebrities or lashed out against migrants and foreign powers.

Trump was extremely skilful at using social media to incite his supporters and mobilize anger and resentment. Trump rarely communicated positive messages but instead produced images of fear, full of doom and conspiracies. All over the globe, countries had joined together to end American dominance. And Washington had not only allowed this to happen but had overseen the process, spending billions overseas while America was falling apart. This needs to stop, and only a person who is not part of the political system can stop it. This person is Trump, a proven winner.

Hitler always said that other parties controlled the press, that they owned or had privileged access to the newspapers and radio. Hitler had nothing, but he won anyway. It is the same with Trump, who defeated the Republican Party and won against all odds. Trump was exceptional at mobilizing the widespread political alienation and said time and again that Clinton was in the pocket of Wall Street, that the political elite in Washington cared only about enriching itself. That Trump is himself part of the 1 per cent is left out of the picture, or, if mentioned, is used as an argument for his success and ability to lead the country. He knows how to make a deal. He has even written a book about it, *The Art of the Deal*, the best business book ever written and on par with the Bible. TV viewers know him as the no-nonsense businessman who gets things done. He is not soft and is focused solely on getting the best deals and winning. He is a proven winner, lives in a latter-day Versailles palace, filled with gold. Trump is a man who simply cannot stop winning.

This is the very reason why he should lead the country. Trump can protect the people. As he puts it in his inauguration speech, 'I will fight for you with every breath in my body – and I will never, ever let you down.' Trump is the protective father who cares for his family-nation. He will never fail America. 'There should be no fear – we are protected, and we will always be protected.'

Trump's programme is to remove everything that can be considered un-American. There is no room for complexity or nuance. We find instead a sharp opposition between hero and the villain, in which violent statements create a dramatic representation of a world divided between 'us' and 'them'. Politics becomes a kind of decontamination process by which the people become the People. Trump appeals to an ideal natural hierarchy that is on the brink of resurrection. 'America' must become great again, and the white man must rule the country and the world. The people shout out for Trump, and he responds in their voice, interpellating the people who reply and gather around the leader. It is a circular process in which Trump is America, and America is Trump. This identification logic resembles that which Claude Lefort uncovered in his analyses of totalitarian ideologies in which there was no space for discussion or disagreement, but in which the nation was the people, and the people were the leader. Hitler is the Nazi movement. The Nazi movement is the Aryan race. And so on. A similar logic is at work in the relationship between Trump and 'America'. Trump *is* the white community he seeks to protect. 'America' is a call to arms. Trump is the incarnation of the dream of the white man who conquers the world. This is Trump's promise to his supporters: things will change yet remain the same. 'We will no longer accept politicians who are all talk and no action – constantly complaining but never doing anything about it. The time for empty talk is over. Now arrives the hour of action.' Trump is the new, he is a recreation of a mystical entity, 'America'. His authority comes from elsewhere, it is not connected to the established political system and its political parties or the administration, it is a higher, spiritual authority. It is an alternative ethical legitimacy. Trump transcends the political system. He is more; he is 'America'.

American rebirth

Trump's speech is filled with temporal markers that concern recreating American greatness. The project is not to 'make America great' or to say 'yes, we can'. It is to 'make America great *again*', to recreate American greatness. The country was great, then it became weak, and now it must become great again. It became weak in part because of Washington but also because of all the un-American elements, the black criminals, the migrants, the Muslims and all the others who undermine the American community. Trump effectively uses the idea of a former greatness that must be recreated. Trump seems to be harking vaguely back to a prosperous post-war golden age in which the USA was the leader of the free world and in which traditional gender roles remained as yet unchallenged. The white man ruled when America was great. Women, blacks and everybody else knew their place, knew that the white man was the natural leader. There were fewer problems back then. Trump can restore social order. Trump's recreation is a promise of clarity. He wishes to return to and recreate the clarity of the post-war era, of the American century. He recollects a time when the United States' military power was a guarantee of safety. Or this, at least, is Trump's vision. A widespread fear of communist spies and nuclear annihilation was, of course, another side to American greatness. Trump promises to turn back the clock, to 'make America great *again*' and return to a period before the Vietnam War, before the civil rights movement, before the black militancy of the 1960s, before political correctness complicated everything.

This rebirth motif is the third fascist feature in Trump's political vocabulary. It fits hand in glove with the two other motifs. The leader must recreate a lost community and remove threats to the nation. We can follow the English fascism historian Roger Griffin in calling this 'palingenetic ultra-nationalism'.[27] The national community overcomes decadence and rises phoenix-like from the ashes, excluding all that is foreign. This motif flows through the inauguration speech and was a constant in the campaign. It remains a continual feature of Trump's narrative of his presidency: make America great again. The foreigners have to go, we will build a wall. Trump is explicit in his threats: he will 'wipe out Islamic terror groups' and 'totally destroy North Korea'. 'America should fight fire with fire.' He jokes to police officers that they should be rougher with subjects and talks about taking the handcuffs off federal immigration agents. Trump has reauthorized local police to get their hands on military equipment. He is certain that torture works and has suggested bringing it back. Trump encouraged an agitated atmosphere at his campaign rallies, at which protesters sometimes got beaten up. Trump's response was always not only to defend the assaults but also to ridicule the victims. His suggestion that 'Second Amendment people' could kill Hillary Clinton if she were elected was part prophesy, part threat. During his campaign, journalists and critical audiences were not only shouted at but physically assaulted. 'Throw them out!' was the chorus, a kind of premonition of worse to come. When a neo-fascist drove his car into an anti-fascist demonstration on 12 August 2017, killing the 32-year-old protester Heather Heyer and wounding 19 other demonstrators, Trump did not denounce the white nationalists, instead condemned 'hatred, bigotry and violence on many sides'. He did not distance himself from the neofascists, preferring to say that there were 'very fine people on both sides'.

Form-giving and exclusion are interwoven processes in Trump's restoration of social order and recreation of the people. The people must be given a clear shape by removing the foreign. 'America First' means recreating the national community by excluding non-Americans and those who are un-American. This is also the purpose of the various protectionist policies presented by Trump's administration, pulling the country out of trade agreements, notably the Pacific Rim trade pact, and tightening import restrictions. His administration has opened investigations into whether China's actions on intellectual property harm the United States, and Trump seems ready to impose the tariffs he promised during his campaign. He has called NATO obsolete but wants allies to pay up, warning that they owe the USA 'massive sums'. As for immigration, Trump still wants to build his wall and is only willing to support legislation to protect hundreds of thousands of immigrants from deportation if the Democrats agree to allocate money for it. He has ended the lottery visa programme; ended extended family-based immigration and signed an executive order that significantly increases the number of immigrants considered a priority for deportation, resulting in federal agents conducting sweeping immigration enforcement raids in several states. Isolation, prosperity and strength are connected for Trump. If America is closed in on itself, it is strong. And rich. And powerful. These are Trump's characteristics too. He is strong, rich and powerful. And he is not afraid to use his powers.

The grim tone of the inauguration speech and its aggressive rhetoric of American carnage is, in itself, an expression of the novelty of the situation. The situation requires something out of the ordinary, and Trump is exceptional, like no other politician. He is a real leader, ready to do what it takes to get America back on track. Throughout his inauguration speech, Trump emphasizes his avant-garde qualities, that he is not your everyday politician.

> Every four years, we gather on these steps to carry out the orderly and peaceful transfer of power...Today's ceremony, however, has very special meaning. Because today we are not merely transferring power from one Administration to another, or from one party to another – but we are transferring power from Washington, DC and giving it back to you, the American people

Those present at the inauguration – itself a big topic of discussion on account of Trump's narcissism – and those who voted for Trump are thus part of something greater, something almost magical. Trump is the charismatic leader in the age of reality television. Trump voters are not only citizens but are on a historical mission. They are part of a movement, 'America', a programme to recreate American greatness. 'Everyone is listening to you now. You came by the tens of millions to become part of a historic movement the likes of which the world has never seen before.'

These body-political connotations also concern Trump himself, who is not only engaged in restoring social order and making America great again but who is himself great and strong. Trump is strength personified. That is why it is necessary for Trump to trash talk all other people, all the time: other candidates during the campaign, members of his own staff, former employees, foreign leaders and journalists, sports stars – they are all weak and silly while Trump is tremendously strong and powerful. This explains why Trump could not accept when, during the campaign, Marco Rubio teased Trump and said he had small hands. Trump kept coming back to the comment, clearly not only frustrated but almost in a kind of panic mode. He just could not stand the suggestion that he was not well hung. 'I have always had people saying: Donald, you have the most beautiful hands. And he referred to my hands, if they are small, something else must be small... I guarantee you, there's no problem.' It was impossible for Trump to ignore Rubio's comment; he just could not accept the suggestion that he had a small penis. It was a humiliation and did not fit the image of the strong and successful businessman. Trump was challenged on his masculinity and could not let it go. It was as though there were a direct link between his political project and his penis. His claim to lead the country was directly related to the size of his manhood. A big penis equals success and power. It is thus obvious that Trump has a big dick. He is a success. That's it. In his own words, 'I'm a very stable genius', 'I'm a winner', and 'I'm incredibly rich'. His opponents, on the other hand, are always weak. Jeb Bush was 'low energy', Ted Cruz was 'the liar Ted', Hillary Clinton was 'the devil' or 'crooked Hillary'. North Korean leader Kim Jong Un is 'short and fat', Meryl Streep is a 'bitch', Whoopi Goldberg is 'terrible', and TV presenter Mika Brzesinski is 'low I.Q. crazy Mika'.

Wherever we look, it is the same story. Trump is strong, and everybody else is weak. Strength equals leadership. Obama was very weak. He was not even born in America but in Kenya and, as such, is un-American. Trump, on the other hand, is white, strong and rich. He is the definition of success, a billionaire reality TV star, a born leader who can fix the situation and make America great again. In Trump's own words:

> We're going to win. We're going to win so much. We're going to win at trade, we're going to win at the border. We're going to win so much, you're going to be sick and tired of winning, you're going to come to me and say, 'Please, please, Mr President, we beg you, we can't win anymore. It's too much.' And I'm going to say 'I'm sorry, but we're going to keep winning, winning, winning. We're going to make America great again.'

Chapter 5

The New Order

If we shelve our initial aversion, and actually listen to Trump, we hear an ultra-nationalist discourse that incites fear and hatred and sees everything as threat. It's about winners and losers, all political conflicts are a question of for or against, everything is black and white. Politics is a competition where the winner takes all.

Whenever fascism begins to leave the ordinary political procedures behind, it is always with the goal of securing a former majority's privileges, a majority that feels threatened, feels like it's losing its grip on power. Trump is restoring white supremacy, extending the American century. There's both cold calculation and desire in Trump's late-capitalist fascism. The white middle class in the USA deals with its own social rout and debt by getting 'its' state to discriminate against others, like the racially oppressed and immigrants. This is Trump's programme, there's plenty of speeches where he talks about the need to create order and hand over more power to the police. And Trump has delivered on his promises by increasing the budget for the military and allowing the police to acquire military equipment. As for immigrants, they can just get back to the 'shithole countries' they came from. Trump is making America great again and this takes the form of exclusion and racism.

Trump is both the original and the new 'America'. He is not in there for a 4-year period, he is heading a much bigger project, as he says in the inaugural address, 'we will determine the course for America and the world for years to come.' The Trump fan is thus part of something bigger, part of a spiritual community intended to last many years. And Trump is dedicated to the project: 'I will fight for you with every breath in my body – and I will never, ever let you down.' There's a spiritual connection between Trump and his supporters that transcends ordinary politics. The two parties represent special interests while Trump's America is a completely different project, a national project. This is why Trump talks about 'total allegiance' to America. America is not something you choose, it is something you live and breathe. As Trump puts it: 'We share one heart, one home, and one glorious destiny.' And, therefore, Trump has no need for a coherent political programme and can promise tax breaks for big companies, cuts in social welfare, as well as jobs and prosperity for the white middle class all at the same time. The most important marker is 'America'. America transcends class differences; the white middle class returns home and becomes part of Trump's white national-capitalist project. At least Trump will secure white families privileged access to what is left job-and-welfare wise, when he is done with his reforms. That's the material incitement, and then there's the pleasure of watching the others suffer.

Trump is a fascist. The way he combines racism and sexism with an idea of an authentic American community that is threatened and needs to be protected by any means cannot be mistaken. His fascism is of course different to Mussolini's fascism and Hitler's Nazism, but it's still fascism. Today it is a late-capitalist fascism that mixes the infantilism of the entertainment industry with ultra-nationalism and makes racist violence funny. Trump is strangely entertaining in all his grotesque intolerance and childish megalomania. The manic insistence on his own superiority and his hateful attacks on women, immigrants and all non-white people only makes sense within the framework of today's trash television and an entertainment culture where the commodity is the only principle of legitimation and where religious superstition and scientific illiteracy long ago replaced any sense of reason or intellectual seriousness. The symbolic production apparatus that was only emerging in the 1930s circulates a mixture of light entertainment and Islamophobia to such an extent that Goebbels would be very proud today. This is US fascism today. It's weirdly funny and at times plain bizarre, but no less dangerous than its predecessors. Like a bad imitation of a car salesman from the 1950s or a character from *Starsky and Hutch* or *Charlie's Angels*.

The fascist solution

It is necessary, as I have tried in the previous chapter, to critically map the fascist ideology that appears in speeches and statements, but it is also important to understand the basis of the new fascism, the reasons for its emergence, in other words to understand the origin of late-capitalist fascism. It's important to describe Trump's rhetoric and show how it is characterized by the presence of fascist tropes, but also to ask structural questions. We need to connect the discourse of fascism to structural socio-economic developments, embedding Trump's speech in a broader historical trajectory. As if the Trump phenomenon is self-explaining, or can be reduced to 'Donald J. Trump' coming on a meteor and destroying the democratic process. He's not, and Trump is not some kind of democratic coup. Reducing Trump to the result of an undemocratic use of democracy tends to confirm Trump's own rhetoric, according to which he is completely different to all the corrupt politicians. We have to analyze Trump's words and policy, but also the longer historical sequence he is part of.

As I explained in the first chapter Trump is to be understood within the framework of a sequence where the financial crisis, the bailout of the banks and the emergence of different kinds of protests are important, but we must also see Trump in a much longer perspective that has to do with the transformations that have been taking place in the US economy since the late 1960s. The English historian Geoff Eley has written about what he calls a fascism producing crisis.[28] Tendencies of breakdown that, so to speak, constitute the conditions of possibility for fascism. If we say fascism is a politics that takes the form of an aggressive nationalism that has to fight off foreign threats, that it is a suspension of so-called democratic discussions and deliberations in favour of an authoritarian state (and war), the question is what kind of crisis makes this sort of political programme possible (and necessary for the preservation of the accumulation of capital)? When does this particular combination of political violence and myth about the nation become appealing or necessary?

If we look at the periods from 1917 to 1922 and 1929 to 1933 in Europe we can, Eley argues, observe the following processes: 1) there's an economic breakdown, 2) that causes the political system to break down, 3) and therefore the population lose confidence in the political system and the political parties. The starting point is thus an economic crisis that becomes a political crisis. And that is the situation today. In the United States of America, but also in Europe, many national parliaments find themselves in a state of paralysis, this is the case in Spain, Italy and Belgium. The financial crisis has thrown them out of course. This is, of course, the development from Brexit to Trump's election. The political institutions are in crisis almost all over the place, and because of that demagogic nationalism thrives. The state has lost its political democratic legitimacy and comes off as the instrument of a small political elite that enriches itself. In a situation of heightened political and economic crisis fascism becomes the solution of a capitalism in distress.

The difference between the interwar period and today is, of course, the First World War; there's no total war on the basis of which political institutions break down. Neither is there an existing international revolutionary movement, as was the case in 1917. But as I argued in the first chapter, there is a scattered mass movement that seems on the brink of discovering previous revolutionary critiques of the capitalist mode of production and the question of its practical abolition. The Arab revolts, the European square occupation movement and the African-American protest movement all point beyond the existing system. If we add in the climate crisis we have a very dramatic situation. The biospheric meltdown undermines the governments' way of doing politics and the fight for resources is intensifying all the time. Confronted with a fight for resources and the continuous growth of the number of climate migrants, states are trying to handle the situation with emergency laws and further militarization.

We are, in other words, in a situation where the political system is no longer functioning and populations are quickly losing their faith in the system, locally and globally. The economic crisis has not been resolved and has become a political crisis – people are leaving the old parties and are voting differently, or just prefer to stay at home – a crisis for the state trapped in neoliberal austerity policy. It is in just such a situation that fascism appears to mediate the re-establishment of political dominance, a solution of contradictions within the capitalist class and the relationship between the classes.

Capitalism's escape attempt

Crisis and breakdown, these are the characteristics of the present situation. This is an ideal milieu for fascism. Fascism is a crisis phenomenon. This was the case in the 1930s and this is the case today. And like in the 1930s, the 'origin' of the new fascism, Trump's fascism, is a financial crisis. That is a steep economic crisis that started in 2007 in the USA and quickly spread to the rest of the world. This is the context. We also, of course, have to factor in the longer historical trajectory of racism in the USA, where Trump is a re-activation of a tradition of white supremacy. A history that includes colonialism, slavery and the class alliance between the white working class and the capitalist class. But the triggering factor is the financial crisis and the resulting disruption. As was the case in the 1930s, where economic crisis spread from the USA to the rest of the capitalist world economy and hit Germany especially hard. The crisis, the 2008 one as well as the long one, dating from the late 1960s, is important and is the backdrop for Trump's narration about a threatened American community and the attempted mobilization of the white American working class.

In a situation of economic crisis fascism appears as a solution that derails real revolutionary alternatives and secures the capitalist mode of production. The basic economic structure always remains untouched. This is the sense in which fascism is counter-revolutionary, it has a rhetoric of regime change but is in fact characterized by a pseudo-revolutionary rhetoric. Think of Trump's attacks on Wall Street. Fascism always gets agitated about the corrupt system, attacking it and claiming to be a restoration of an original order, but it always protects capital. Fascism is, in that way, a revolution against the revolution. It appropriates language and slogans from anti-capitalism but embeds them in a nationalist narrative where the fundamental contradictions of capitalism remain invisible and are replaced with a focus on racial and cultural differences. The anti-systemic rhetoric and attacks against neoliberal globalization are thus in fact an expression of a fight within capitalism that has to do with different factions wanting to steer the economy. In that sense fascism is counter-revolutionary and is not at all interested in initiating fundamental change but instead wants to secure the privileges of certain groups who fear social declassification and – very importantly – make sure that any kind of capital-negating get-go is eliminated, derailing potential revolutionary perspectives.

It is important to derail alternatives and it is important to control and tighten security, prevent things from getting out of hand (in the sense of a larger socio-material transformation). The crisis needs to be steered; in the 1930s the answer was a strong state power that could intervene and steer the economic processes. Steer them with a view to securing private property and removing unions and working-class organizations, keeping wages low and creating demand, and subsidizing industry, effectively ending unemployment (as well as removing all non-Aryan subjects). This policy was the basis for the collaboration between leading capitalist groups in Germany and the Nazi party. Capital depended on the Nazi state's ability to create demand. The solution to the economic crisis was a command economy, where the state created demand and kept wages low. In the Nazi war economy profits were high and wages low. In that way, the capitalist economy was not only saved, the revolutionary working-class movement was destroyed. As Italian Left communist Amadeo Bordiga writes, fascism was preparation for the slaughter of the European wage slaves in the Second World War. Capitalism was saved, the rights guaranteed by the bourgeois state temporarily suspended and the revolutionary threat negated.[29]

Already in the mid-1930s, the German Marxist economist Alfred Sohn-Rethel described how the state took over the dispositive function of the employer, restructuring the economy by demanding war material.[30] Today we would probably call it a bailout. German capital's debt was 'socialized' through the state. The war economy created a financial deficit for the state – a drop in exports and a rising need for imports of raw materials and consumer commodities – that ended up making imperial expansion necessary. The economic side of the crisis was thus solved through 'artificial' demand, militarization and armament (and later war) and the political crisis was resolved through the establishment of Nazi party dictatorship. If fascism is a crisis solution model for capitalism, it is a highly particular one where politics tends to become autonomous. German capital handed over political power to the Nazi party in return for the ability to appropriate politically produced profits. Bourgeois democracy was temporarily suspended in order to save capital.

The crisis made fascism necessary. There are of course obvious parallels to the situation in the United States today where the so-called neoliberal accumulation regime has to be replaced with something new, the economic crisis has become a political crisis and there's a growing need for political and economic change. Trump promises change. And his election is a victory for that part of the local capitalist class that has lost on globalization and finds it difficult to operate on the world market. It is the nationalist and protectionist faction of US industry that is now running the economy. US economic policy will be dominated by protectionism on the world market, deregulation and tax relief for companies and the launch of largescale infrastructure projects. The budget for the US military has already been raised by more than 10 per cent. The plan is to help the companies that find it difficult to compete in the global economy.

Globalization and trade deals are replaced by protectionism and possibly by trade wars. The election of Trump marks a defeat for the most internalized part of US capital, from now on the nation has to be protected against inner and outer enemies. Protectionism walks hand in hand with an ultra-nationalist discourse according to which all strangers are enemies. Trump will not spend money on geopolitical hegemony unless it is visible on the bottom line and benefits American capital. 'Law and order' at home and 'cold peace' abroad. America is going to win again through cancelling trade agreements, by getting rid of immigrants, closing the borders for Muslims, by throwing more African Americans in prison and by giving the local police free rein to control the surplus population. This is the project of late-capitalist fascism.

Chaos in Washington

Trump is trying to fulfil many of his campaign promises. It has proven difficult, but he is slowly getting there, dropping climate change as a national threat and replacing judges on all levels, imposing the Muslim ban time and again, ejecting immigrants in large numbers, cutting taxes and working hard to destroy

Obama Care, pulling out of international organizations and rescinding deportation protection for hundreds of thousands of people, announcing a move of the US embassy to Jerusalem and threatening both North Korea and Iran. After a year, it is still not clear how much Trump will be able to achieve as president, but he seems intent on doing his best at creating an extremely volatile political atmosphere, where he attacks the media and the judiciary and different parts of the administration. For a long time he simply preferred to have an empty administration, keeping many crucial US government jobs unfilled. But he has also been busy firing the ones he appoints whenever they appear 'weak'. The list is already long: Michael Flynn, Sean Spicer, Reince Priepus, Anthony Scaramucci and Sebastian Gorka were all kicked out, and even Bannon left. His administration is a chaotic beehive of competing factions unable to collaborate. But this is the way it is supposed to be. Trump prefers chaos.

The news is of course just 'fake news', the media are not just dishonest, 'they are the most dishonest people on earth'. Trump recently announced a Dishonest Media Awards. The media are 'enemies of the American people'. If someone believed that Trump would change his discourse once he was in the White House, they were mistaken. The rhetoric from the campaign has just continued. Racism, sexism and ultra-nationalism are still the ingredients of Trump's American greatness.

It has been difficult for Trump to repeal the Affordable Care Act, but he is still working on it, and is slowly pulling it apart, no matter the cost for poor and sick people in the USA. The travel ban has had its own life, Trump has tried to impose it several times only to be met with protests and legal challenges. Trump has targeted what he calls Muslim countries, and the meaning of the ban is clear for everybody to see. Trump wants to get rid of the terrorists (read Muslims). Muslims and immigrants have to go. Not only immigrants from 'terrorist countries' but also immigrants from African 'shithole countries' and places like Haiti and other Central American countries. As Trump put it in a meeting in the Oval Office in January 2018: 'Why are we having all these people from shithole countries come here?', suggesting bringing immigrants from Norway instead. 'Why do we need more Haitians? Take them out.'

The proposed 2,000-mile long wall to Mexico has yet to be built, but Trump is trying hard to get funding for it from Congress. The initial phase of the border wall will cost 18 billion US dollars. The money is to go towards 316 miles of new fencing and reinforcing 400 miles of existing barriers. If Trump succeeds, more than half of the border with Mexico will have a wall by 2027. And against all evidence Trump continues to claim that Mexico will pay for the wall. 'I believe Mexico will pay for the wall. I have a very good relationship with Mexico. But yes, in some form, Mexico will pay for the wall.'

It is impossible to keep up with Trump and his bizarre racist and misogynist rants. But it is important not to get caught in an analysis where we compare Trump to some kind of imagined normality before Trump, as if Trump's fascism is the exact opposite of the policies pursued by Bush and Obama. That Trump is a fascist does not mean that Bush Junior, Obama or Hillary Clinton and Bernie Sanders somehow incarnate democracy. And that all we have to do is remove Trump and get back to some 'before Trump' situation. The crisis was already there. Trump has merely accelerated it, no doubt he has, but there is no 'normality' to return to. That is the shocking truth that Trump reveals. So it's not that easy unfortunately, opposing Trump in favour of 'normal' politicians and supporting democracy. Fascism is not the opposite of democracy, fascism emerges in crisis-ridden national democracies when there's a need to create order and prevent alternatives from emerging. Fascism is thus not an anomaly but a possibility in any national democracy. And when democracy as a political form is embedded in a nation state there's always the risk that national democracy closes on itself and wants to protect its citizens from what it perceives as external threats. The national home is threatened and has to be made safe and orderly. Fascism is, in other words, an immanent to national democracies. Hitler and Mussolini did not dissolve democracy, they undermined it from within by making it incapable of functioning, thus creating a need for a strong leader who has to clean up and restore order. Trump does not need paramilitary troops in the streets, Trump is fully capable of creating legislative chaos himself and thus undermining existing political authority, producing the need for a different kind of authority, an authentic American authority, that being Trump himself of course. The first year of Trump's presidency shows that he is leading through chaos. This is late-capitalist fascism at work, it's messy and overwhelming. Planned chaos.

Chapter 6

Neither Trump, Nor Democracy

Whither democracy after Trump? The election victory and current presidency of Donald J. Trump makes it relevant to raise the question of democracy once again. In many ways, Trump appears as a democratic coup, in which democracy is hijacked by a populist television celebrity and construction tycoon. In this view, Trump is perceived as a threat to democracy. His fight against the media and the courts has moved many a commentator, such as the American feminist philosopher Judith Butler, to paint a picture of Trump as a confrontation between right-wing nationalism and democracy.

But, unfortunately, there is no populist, totalitarian or fascist excess, if by that we understand something essentially different from national-democratic normality. The opposition between populism/fascism and democracy, in which anti-fascist and democratic mobilization becomes the answer to Trump, is a short circuit that excludes alternatives by invoking the status quo, which has long since shown itself to be an exception.[31] The fate of the black population in the USA or refugees and migrants in/on their way to Europe testify to this.

The populism analysis is, in other words, bad. Simply stated, the argument is that Trump the populist appeals to the people in a suspect manner, his explicitly nationalist rhetoric short circuits representative democracy and clears the way for racist, misogynist and Islamophobic policies. Beyond any doubt, Trump's political programme is ultra-nationalist and takes the shape of a late-capitalist fascism, based on the exclusion of all that is 'non-American', including everything from external threats, such as Muslims and Mexicans, to internal threats, such as black people and feminists. However, the problem with the populism analysis is that it so clearly affirms democracy: it leaves the mainstream as, well, mainstream; as the infallible norm, which it is better to defend and to follow. In this way, the opposition becomes the democrats against the populists, in which populism is the bad, the absence of arguments and a mobilization of the worst in the soul of the people, while democracy is the good, which we must defend. Democracy is good, even though the wrong candidate was elected.

As Giorgio Agamben has shown in his comprehensive *Homo sacer* project, the truth, however, is that there is an intimate link between democracy and fascism.[32] Democracy depends on a founding ambiguity, by which democracy means both the power of the people, and government, the form through which power is legitimated and the manner in which it is exercised. Democracy is the movement between these two poles. As formulated by Agamben, democracy is the carrier of a biopolitical class struggle, which is constantly threatening to break out. Indeed, it constantly does. The so-called refugee crisis in Europe is a good example; the EU and European nation states have turned the Mediterranean into an enormous mass grave, and are doing anything possible to prevent refugees from entering Europe. All of this happens under the guise of perfectly respectable democracy.

In the West of today, democracy equals national democracy – representative democracy with its political parties, elections and formations of government is rooted in a nation state, with all the racist radicalization and rule by decree through a state of exception this makes possible. In the course of the last 2 decades, we have been witness to the ways in which these national democracies have stepped up the fight against terror, which is constantly invoked when restricting civil liberties and criminalizing forms of political protest, and most of all in the desperate attempt to prevent refugees and migrants setting foot on European soil. The border regime, which has been built up in the EU these last 25 years, but also in Australia and the USA, is pre-Trump evidence of the fascist dimension of nation-state democracy, in which some lives are identified as an external virus, threatening the national community, and are consequently subjugated and treated as inferior. The authoritarian turn, which Trump represents, is therefore already present. The need, constantly expounded, to protect 'our' culture trumps everything. We can push the formulation in order to say: Trump is already present in European refugee policy.

In the period between the two world wars, Karl Korsch described the relationship between fascism and democracy.[33] For Korsch, there was no essential difference between the bourgeois democracies and fascism. There was, rather, an internal connection, precisely that bourgeois democracy has an inherently fascist dimension. Because of this, Korsch did not want to abstractly oppose fascism with democracy. As he drily remarked, a modern electoral system – with town halls and debates, elections and so on – never stopped the creation of concentration camps or prevented fascism. Every democratic country has or can get its own Dachau, Korsch wrote. Thus, defending democracy in order to avoid an authoritarian turn does not work. It never has. This was crucial for Korsch. It does not mean that Korsch relativized the horrors of Nazism. The point is that in certain situations democracies 'voluntarily' commit suicide because they prefer law and order to disorder, no matter how brutal and murderous this order is. This was, according to Korsch, the situation in 1922 Italy as well as in 1933 Germany.

The conclusion to the analysis of both Korsch and Agamben is this: it is a mistake to put democracy opposite fascism or suggest a popular front to defend democracy against Trump's fascism. As the council communist Korsch and the Italian philosopher Agamben teach us, this is to misunderstand the founding ambiguity of national democracy, by which fascism is an immanent possibility, and not an external threat. The fact is that in a state of emergency, it is possible for national democracy to tone down its democratic dimension and ratchet up the national dimension, and thereby intensify its exclusionary logic, which has all along been working in hiding and on the margins (in the colonies or on the border). This is exactly what we see happening with Trump.

The naturalness of democracy

The mobilization to defend democracy tells us a lot about democracy today. As a starting point, we are all democrats, of that there is, naturally, no doubt. Democracy is unconditionally a positive. Traditionally, democracy is defined as a form of government in which the people decide. Democracy is majority rule. That's democracy as opposed to aristocracy, in which an elite decide, or oligarchy, in which the strongest are in charge. In democracy, the people have the power. That would be the trimmed-down, simple definition. But, if we make a list of democracies and politicians who claim to be democrats and be for democracy, we will quickly find that democracy is, perhaps, not such a coherent thing as we normally consider it to be. Politicians as different as Evo Morales, Angela Merkel, Robert Mugabe, Lars Løkke Rasmussen, Raúl Castro, Thaksin Shinawatra, Vladimir Putin and our friend, Donald Trump, all define themselves as democrats, and North Korea and China as well as the USA and Denmark, but also Morocco and Iran, understand themselves as democratic states with regular elections, albeit of rather different types. In other words, if we start taking a closer look at the many different democracies that exist today, we quickly find that the term democracy lacks substance. It quickly becomes clear, one is tempted to say, that democracy is a rubber stamp, which can approve very different content. If we look at the real world, and examine Denmark, Norway, but also Turkey and, let's say, Indonesia, we quickly find that there is no single democracy, and that democracy does not equal a single specific type of government, nor a specific political culture. It is more likely a multiplicity of overlapping and contradictory regimes, institutions and ways of life.

However, what is surprising is that this multiplicity does not really challenge the discourse of democracy. Today, all the different, often contradictory types of democracy actually only seem to confirm the importance of democracy. No one is leaving the club for this reason. We are all always already democrats. Rather than being emptied of meaning or appearing problematic, the concept seems to float above the waters. It is not really troubled by the various exceptions. Rather, it is exactly its exceptions or 'mistakes' that seem to confirm the idea of democracy. North Korea and Mugabe are 'local conditions', they are details that do not disturb the total image. That there are both democratic constitutional monarchies (Denmark), republican democracies (France), as well as apartheid democracies (Israel), military democracies (Egypt), state communist democracies (North Korea) and even imperial democracies (Japan), does not appear to truly matter. The idea of democracy is not weakened or undermined by its concrete variations, it only appears to become more important. The exceptions are in some way already included in the idea of democracy, which does not suffer from the polysemy, but still manages to appear as a universal principle. We are all democrats today.

In this sense, 'democracy' is the very heart of the political discourse of today, the automatic go-to thing. It is a magical word, an incantation that does not only start political processes, but also endows events and actions with meaning. *For* democracy; Against Trump. The word is used all the time. We understand it intuitively. Hence the automatic: 'we are all democrats'. What would the opposite of this even be?

But behind the apparent and self-evident, there lies a hidden multiplicity or absence of meaning. Because actually, democracy does not really mean anything. That is, of course it does. The term connotes a lot, but way too much. It means way too many things at the same time. But, even though it is not consistent, does not make a coherent object, and points in all possible directions, it is nevertheless the keyword of the present epoch. It determines a horizon and *is* the epoch. Our epoch. In reality, democracy equals the *suspension* of the political and not the *implementation* of the political. Democracy is the most important political term, but it is incoherent. It first and foremost functions as an annulment of any possible challenge to the current mixture of national democracy and capitalism.

The best idea in the world

Democracy is the best, that's how it is. Everybody is for democracy, and the support for democracy transcends any political opposition. Republicans and Democrats in the USA, The Red-Green Alliance and Danish People's Party in Denmark, everyone is for democracy. Of course, this has a lot to do with how democracy within the last couple of decades has become the opposite of terrorism. A funny expression of the success of democracy can be found in the poll that *Morgenavisen Jyllands-Posten* carried out in 2014, in which democracy came in first followed by freedom and love.

In November 2014, the newspaper asked its readers to elect 'the best idea in the world'. The winner of the poll was democracy. The poll took place in connection with the publication of the anthology *50 ideer der ændrede verden* [50 Ideas that Changed the World], edited by the former value form theorist Hans-Jørgen Schanz, published by Aarhus University Press.[34] In the weeks leading up to the announcement of the winner, which took place on 9 November – a date with great historical significance: the Fall of the Wall – the paper had presented various candidates to the title of the best idea in the world. Tolerance, love, the market, the soul, the nation, truth, happiness, art, rationality and 40 other ideas. But it was democracy that ran away with the title. Love and freedom came in runners up. But democracy was the best idea in the world, according to the 926 of *Jyllands-Posten*'s readers who cast a vote.[35]

The poll tells us much about democracy today. First and foremost, of course, that democracy is something good. Nothing less than the best idea in the world. Of course, it was no great part of the paper's readership that took part in the poll, with a circulation of 100,000, 926 is not very many, but democracy did come in first.

When the competition was launched in *Jyllands-Posten*, all the 50 ideas were listed and briefly explained. About democracy it was stated that:

> Aristotle and Plato found democracy to be a bad idea. Nevertheless, Ancient Greece was the cradle of democracy. It lasted for 300 years, before it was overruled by powerful men, and did not come back into play before the struggle of the people against absolutism in the seventeenth century.

In this description, not only is the historical perspective dominant, it doesn't say a lot about democracy today. The myth of Greece as the cradle of democracy and the struggle against absolutism are what is described. There is not a lot about the historical development since 'the struggle of the people against absolutism'. Perhaps this is an expression of how democracy has conquered in the West; even though Mihail Larsen, author of the article on democracy in Schanz's anthology, does write that democracy 'is not just something you have, it is something for which you must fight', the threats against democracy are only described as coming from the outside.

It is interesting that it was *Jyllands-Posten* that set up the poll in collaboration with Aarhus University Press. Of course, there are practical explanations of 'local' character involved; the paper's offices are in Viby, outside Aarhus, where the university press is, naturally, also located. So, it was an obvious collaboration and everybody got something out of it, the publisher a lot of attention for the book and the paper content for its culture and debate section. But that it is precisely *Jyllands-Posten* and its readers who elect democracy as the best idea in the world is still interesting, given the history of that newspaper. In the 1920s and 1930s, *Jyllands-Posten* expressed its unconditional support first for Mussolini and then later Hitler:

> Mussolini saved Italy from the communist flood, for which a useless parliamentary government had made it ripe, and no one can question that his dictatorship has been a blessing for the Italian people. Germany was faced with a similar catastrophe when Hitler made his way to power.

It is funny how the readers now choose democracy as the best idea, but then, the 1930s have long gone. Or have they? In collaboration with the tabloid press, *Jyllands-Posten* played an important part in the Islamophobic turn in Danish politics during the second half of the 1990s, with countless articles on asylum seekers cheating the Danish welfare system. And later, of course, the paper became the centre of the so-called Muhammad cartoon crisis, when the paper wanted to give an extra notch to the bullying of Muslims living here by depicting their prophet as a terrorist and pimp.

If, in connection with the poll in *Jyllands-Posten*, one was to attach a caption to the image of democracy in the West today, 'self-evident' would be a good suggestion. Today, we are all democrats, even if we are actually xenophobes. We bully Muslims living here, and do everything possible to prevent migrants coming and receiving asylum, but nevertheless democracy is a universal value, it is simply the best idea in the world. Today, we are all national-democrats, we all support democracy (and the nation state). Only a vanishingly small minority will proclaim to be against democracy. To do so would be to exclude yourself from any political debate. Democracy: yes, naturally. Supposedly only people such as Abu al-Baghdadi from IS are against.

In other words, democracy appears so natural today, that it is seemingly against nature to even consider an alternative. If something is not democratic, then it is because it has yet to become democratic. There are no alternatives, only a lack of democracy. In this way, democracy is an ideology, one which has now lost foundation in history and has grown to seem natural or to be an eternal good. A mythology, we might call it, with Roland Barthes, or a ruling representation with Guy Debord, that is, a regulating concept, which in an active sense governs patterns of behaviour and establishes structures of solidarity, creates the world in its image. To be against democracy is thus to be against all that is right. In this way, we can say that democracy is the insurmountable horizon of society; there is nothing behind or next to democracy. It is not only unquestioned, it is self-evident. It is simply the best.

The poll in *Jyllands-Posten* is in itself an expression of a development, in which democracy has become part of an extended culture of participation, where everyone is active and encouraged to participate and make their voice heard. *Just do it!* Jodi Dean reads such tendencies as the emergence of a communicative capitalism, where democracy is another word for self-exploitation. Exemplary of this development is when computer and mobile phone companies like Apple and Telia make use of a democratic rhetoric of inclusion and participation and understand consumers as users and participants.[36] Participation is the solution to everything. Dean sees this development as an expression of an appropriation of a once transgressive and critical position, by which new political subjects such as students, women and migrants claimed self-determination and autonomy. However, this critique was turned upside down, it was turned into precarious labour and self-determination at work. The demands of autonomy and creativity became a blurring of the lines between work and leisure. Democracy became an environment, and – for the privileged few – the never-ending succession of life-style choices.

(Capitalist) equality

Today, democracy appears indistinguishable from capitalism, they are inseparable and presented as the condition of each other's possibility. Alain Badiou terms it capitalo-parliamentarism.[37] For Badiou, democracy today is simply an expression of 'political impotence'. Today, democratic ideology functions in reality as a smokescreen for the oligarchic structures of the economy.

In the 1840s, the young Marx described how political democracy goes hand in hand with the capitalist mode of production, and actually helps to hide its brutal hunt for profit.[38] Democracy makes it appear as if there is political equality, as if the voice of a homeless person and a billionaire are actually of equal worth. But in capitalism, political equality, of course, covers an actual social inequality. In capitalist society, politics is a separate sphere in which power can circulate and even allow itself to be critiqued and challenged, without the material conditions of society being challenged. There is no meaningful relation between the socio-economical hierarchy and the political sphere, political identities are separated from socio-economic status, and political equality can easily co-exist with social exploitation and class inequality. This way, in the separate sphere of politics, the citizens can live out the fiction of equality, as long as they pretend as if they were equal, as if riches, income, work and hierarchies did not matter. The conflicts of social inequality are in this way suspended or 'forgotten' in the political sphere. At the ballot box (and in front of the commodity) we are all equal.

A brief history of (late) democracy

The chorus is always that democracy is good. We don't even need to debate that. But, we also know that democracy is at the same time a strange, amorphous thing. It is the most important value of all; we do not compromise on democracy. But then, we do it all the time anyway. At least, we have done so several times these last couple of decades. The peculiar process in late November 2000, by which George Bush Jr became US president even though he had lost the election, was a fine example. To arrive at the Bush victory, the Supreme Court decided that the votes from Florida were *not* to be recounted. Yes, only a minority of Americans vote in elections, and the entire process of states and the electoral colleges often result in the inauguration of presidents with the fewer votes, which is not so democratic to begin with, but still, this was the first time that the American national democracy became the stage of a veritable coup in which the counting of votes was outright prohibited (and thus the election of Al Gore as president was avoided).

The next example is provided by the same Bush, who after 9/11 increased the repressive side of the state and showed how small a contradiction there is between the occasional (and, given Florida 2000, somewhat selective) election procedures of national democracy and government in a state of exception, with all that includes of state terror at home, war abroad and an extensive system of torture. In reply to the attacks on The World Trade Center and The Pentagon, Bush declared 'war on terror' and suspended a number of civil rights in order to preserve the nation state. The Patriot Act and similar legislation undermined several of the founding principles of the rule of law, and made it possible for the American military to capture and detain people indefinitely. Thereby, a space between law and exception was opened, and could be used in various manners. The Guantanamo camp in Cuba is an example of how such a space works. Here, the sovereign detains subjects who are said to be a threat to the nation. These subjects are deprived of their legal rights and exempted from the alternatives of international law – they are neither prisoners of war nor criminals who may have their cases tried in court. Democratic politics are, in this way, changed step by step into a continual security operation, in which the citizens' civil rights can be suspended by reference to the threat of terror.

In the course of the financial crisis as well, we saw various examples of how interesting displacements may occur when oppositions between national democracy and the economy arise. In Greece and Italy, elected politicians were removed and replaced with financiers and former employees of the European Central Bank. What happened in Greece is quite telling: first the Prime Minister of Greece, George Papandreou, announced a referendum on the crisis package that the EU and IMF offered the country, then he was put in his place by Merkel and Sarkozy and forced to cancel the referendum, only then to step down and hand over the position to Lucas Papademos, the former vice president of the European Central Bank. A number of elections followed, at the end of which the neo-eurocommunist party SYRIZA formed a government with the mandate to renegotiate the terms of the crisis package. But the European Central Bank refused to change anything at all, and chose to close their ears to the wishes of the Greek population completely. The conclusion is, of course, that democracy is fine and all that, but there are other matters that are more important.

The image-political take on this gradual emptying of the political is, of course, that the constantly increasing flow of images and representations hides the fundamental emptiness of democracy. In representative democracies, the real function of elections, as Cornelius Castoriadis writes, is not to allow the people to choose, but to equip them with the idea that the problems of society are much too complicated and best left to the political parties and the state.[39] The election is a ritual endowing a certain model of society with visual consistency. It is important to catch the interest of the people, so whatever content remains in the empty shape of the ritual evaporates. Democracy is caught between wanting to pacify the voters – don't worry we will an-

swer all the complex questions – and at the same time prefera-
bly not vanquish them completely, so that they lose trust in the
system. Therefore, elections become more and more spectacular,
voters are consumers of political decisions. The actual struggle,
of course, takes place elsewhere. What is important is not the debate in front of rolling cameras by the candidates we may choose
between, the actual struggle takes place earlier, ensuring that
the question of the unsuitability of the nation state itself, but, of
course, also private property and money, is never formulated.
Some questions can never be posed inside the framework of national democracy.

'The People'

Trump ought to be given occasion for examining national democracy, because it is within this framework that he became
president, but unfortunately this seldom occurs. Actually, most
analysis unfolds in a manner that precisely avoids analysis of
national democracy. One way in which this happens is to use
the concept of populism and then blame 'the people' for voting
the wrong way. In other words, the problem is the people, not
democracy. But, in fact, it is the democratic system, which, so
to say, creates 'the people', who are then faced with a choice
(Clinton v Trump). So, it is not the people who elect Trump, but
rather the representative national democracy which produces
the people as the voting subject, as Jacques Rancière writes.[40]
The founding operation in representative democracy is not the
choice between the various candidates, mapped onto an historically handed down, but rather arbitrary scale going from left to
right, but the production of the people as the political subject.
However, this operation is not really visible. Since the people
vote and choose this or that candidate, it appears as if this act is
the actual political action, as if it is the most important gesture in
democracy. But it is not. The production of the people is prior to
this. With Althusser, we may call it an interpellation, a complex

operation whereby a subject with agency and self-awareness is produced, one which sees itself as the starting point of political action, but in reality is an effect of a structure.[41] In this case, representative democracy is more about the people retrospectively giving power to an individual or a party, than the people having political agency or electing someone.

The foundational operation of representative national democracy is to produce the people, which then successively gives its votes to the advantage of one or the other candidate. The election makes it appear as if the people have power and elect a president or parliament, but it is actually the other way around. In the US, the election in November was between Trump and Clinton (we forget for a moment that there were other candidates, not least Jill Stein of the Green Party), a flamboyant billionaire, construction tycoon and reality star, and a former First Lady and Secretary of State. That is, two candidates who only with great difficulty can be seen as expressions of the American people. So, the process is the other way around, the democratic system creates the people. In other words, it is Trump who effectively has produced (a particular representation of) the American people, not the American people who have chosen Trump.

The election of Trump occurred against the backdrop of the transformation of politics into administration, which has occurred over the last 3 decades, where progressively more areas have been left to the ravaging of market forces. In this process, Trump appears as a different brand, more ready and willing to advance racist and protectionist solutions. He marks a difference. But there is, of course, at the same time also continuity, in that the USA, in Joel Olson's words, has always been and is still a white democracy, where all are equal in principle, but white people more so than everyone else.[42] Equality and privilege go hand in hand in the USA. From 1607 to 1965 citizenship was a racial privilege in the USA, and to this day white people are equipped with invisible, unearned privileges from which they can retain or improve their situation. On paper, the USA is a colour-blind society, whiteness is no longer a state-sanctioned distinction, but in reality, the USA is still characterized by white supremacy. This is clear from all the statistics, whether they are on infant mortality, incarceration, stop and search, education, housing, riches or unemployment. The election of Trump confirms this situation, and only an end to whiteness as a socio-political category can create the conditions of possibility for an American democracy. That would almost be half a revolution. The whole revolution would occur when the critique of national democracy – the process of destitution – is combined with the critique of capitalism. This is the programme. There is plenty to be done for the anti-nationalist forces.

Endnotes

1. Perry Anderson: 'Why the System Will Still Win', in: *Le Monde diplomatique*, March 2017, pp. 6-7.

2. Paul Krugman: 'Secular Stagnation, Coalmines, Bubbles, and Larry Summers', in: *The New York Times*, 16 November 2013; http://krugman.blogs.nytimes.com/2013/11/16/secular-stagnation-coalmines-bubbles-and-larry-summers/; Immanuel Wallerstein: 'Structural Crisis: Or Why Capitalists Might No Longer Find Capitalism Rewarding', Immanuel Wallerstein, Craig Calhoun and Michael Mann (eds.): *Does Capitalism Have a Future?* (Oxford: Oxford University Press, 2013), pp. 9-36.

3. Insurgent Notes: 'We're Tempted to Say We Told You So, But We Won't', in: *Insurgent Notes*, no. 14, 2016; http://insurgentnotes.com/2016/11/were-tempted-to-say-we-told-you-so-but-we-wont/

4. Robert Brenner: *The Economics of Global Turbulence: The Advanced Capitalist Economies from Long Boom to Long Downturn, 1945-2005* (London and New York: Verso, 2006).

5. For a description of the wave of protests, see my *Crisis to Insurrection* (Wivenhoe: Minor Compositions, 2015).

6. It was British cultural historian Mark Fisher who described the period after the fall of the Wall as 'capitalist realism', in which it was no longer possible to imagine another world. Capitalism had become the only reality. See Mark Fisher: *Capitalist Realism: Is there no Alternative* (London: Zero Books, 2009).

7. Frank B. Wilderson, III: 'The Prison Slave as Hegemony's (Silent) Scandal', in: *Social Justice*, vol. 30, no. 2, 2003, pp. 18-27.

8. See Michelle Alexander: *The New Jim Crow: Mass Incarceration in the Age of Colorblindness* (New York: The New Press,

2010).

9. Reading Trump as counter-revolutionary draws on classic analyses of counter-revolution, especially Karl Korsch's articles of the 1920s and 1930s (collected in Douglas Kellner (ed.): *Karl Korsch: Revolutionary Theory* (Austin & London: University of Texas Press, 1977)), Arno J Mayer's *Dynamics of Counterrevolution in Europe, 1879-1956: An Analytic Framework* (New York: Harper & Row, 1971) and Herbert Marcuse's *Counterrevolution and Revolt* (Boston: Beacon Press, 1972). Marx's *The Eighteenth Brumaire of Louis Bonaparte* is, of course, in many ways the touchstone for any analysis of counter-revolution.

10. Mike Davis: 'Election 2016', in: *New Left Review*, no. 103, 2017, pp 5-8; Naomi Klein: 'It was the Democrats' Embrace of Neoliberalism that Won it for Trump', in: *The Guardian*, 9 November 2016, https://www.theguardian.com/commentisfree/2016/nov/09/rise-of-the-davos-class-sealed-americas-fate; Nancy Fraser: 'The End of Progressive Neoliberalism', in: *Dissent Magazine*, 2 January 2017, https://www.dissentmagazine.org/online_articles/progressive-neoliberalism-reactionary-populism-nancy-fraser

11. For a critique of the term neoliberalism, see Carsten Juhl: 'Critique of the Term Neoliberalism' on *Mute*, 24 March 2017, http://www.metamute.org/community/your-posts/critique-term-neoliberalism

12. Cf. Walter Benjamin: 'The Work of Art in the Age of Its Mechanical Reproducibility' [1936], in: Benjamin: *The Work of Art in the Age of Its Mechanical Reproducibility, and Other Writings on Media* (Cambridge, MA & London: Belknap Press, 2000), pp. 19-55; Guy Debord: *The Society of the Spectacle* [1967] (New York: Zone Books, 1995).

13. Claude Lefort: 'The Question of Democracy', in: Lefort: *Democracy and Political Theory* [1986] (MIT Press, 1989), p. 11.

14. George Seeßlen: *Trump! Populismus als Politik* (Berlin: Bertz +

Fischer, 2017).

15. Michael Rogin: *Ronald Reagan, the Movie and Other Episodes in Political Demonology*, Berkeley (Los Angeles and London: University of California Press, 1987).

16. Many of the best fascism researchers have written short commentaries on Trump, both before and after the election in November 2016. Some of the best include: Jane Caplan: 'Trump and Fascism: A View from the Past', *History Workshop blog*, 17 November 2016, http://www.historyworkshop.org.uk/trump-and-fascism-a-view-from-the-past/, Mark Mazover: 'Ideas That Fed the Beast of Fascism Flourish Today', in *Financial Times*, 6. 11, 2016; and Robert Steigmann-Gall: 'What the American Left Doesn't Understand about Fascism', in: *Huffington Post*, 10 June 2016. See also the interview with Robert O Paxton on Democracy Now, 15 March 2016, https://www.democracynow.org/2016/3/15/father_of_fascism_studies_donald_trump

17. Ian Kershaw: *Hitler* (London: Penguin, 2008).

18. Robert O Paxton: *The Anatomy of Fascism* (New York: Alfred A Knopf, 2004).

19. Walter Benjamin: 'The Work of Art in the Age of Mechanical Reproduction' [1939], https://www.marxists.org/reference/subject/philosophy/works/ge/benjamin.htm

20. Alice Yager Kaplan: *Reproductions of Banality: Fascism, Literature and French Intellectual Life* (Minneapolis and London: University of Minnesota Press, 1986), pp. 25-35.

21. Enzo Traverso: *Les nouveaux visages du fascisme* (Paris: Textuel, 2017).

22. Georges Bataille: 'The Psychological Structure of Fascism' [1932], in: *New German Critique*, no. 16, 1979, pp. 64-87.

23. WEB Du Bois: *Black Reconstruction in America* (New York: Free Press, 1962). Following Du Bois, historians such as Noel Ignatiev and David Roediger have given detailed analyses of the splitting up of the American working class, of how

Irish and Italian migrant workers bettered their positions by distancing themselves from black workers, thereby affirming a white working-class identity. Noel Ignatiev: *How the Irish Became White* (London and New York: Routledge, 1995) and David Roediger: *The Wages of Whiteness: Race and the Making of the American Working Class* (London and New York: Verso, 1999).

24. Georges Sorel wrote about myth in the book *Reflections on Violence* [1908] (Cambridge and New York: Cambridge University Press, 1999).

25. Giorgio Agamben: *Means without End* [1995] (Minneapolis and London: University of Minnesota Press, 2000), p. 29.

26. *Means without End*, p. 31.

27. Roger Griffin: *The Nature of Fascism* (London and New York: Routledge, 1991).

28. Geoff Eley: 'Fascism Then and Now', in: *Socialist Register 2016* (London: Merlin Press, 2016), pp. 91-117.

29. Amadeo Bordiga: 'War and Revolution', 1950, https://libcom.org/library/war-revolution-amadeo-bordiga

30. Alfred Sohn-Rethel: *The Economy and Class Structure of German Fascism* [1973], (London: Free Association Books, 1987).

31. Judith Butler: 'A Statement from Judith Butler', *e-flux* conversations, 11 November 2016; http://conversations.e-flux.com/t/a-statement-from-judith-butler/5215

32. Giorgio Agamben: *Homo sacer. Sovereign Power and Bare Life* (Stanford: Stanford University Press, 1998).

33. Karl Korsch: *Marxism, State and Counterrevolution* (Amsterdam and Hannover: Offizin Verlag & Internationaal instituut voor sociale geschiedenis, 2018).

34. Hans-Jørgen Schanz (ed.): *50 ideer der ændrede verden* (Aarhus: Aarhus Universitetsforlag, 2014).

35. Lars From and Klaus Dohm: 'Læserkåring: Demokrati er verdens bedste ide', in: *Jyllands-Posten*, 9 November 2014, pp. 6-7.

36. Jodi Dean: *Democracy and other Neoliberal Fantasies: Communicative Capitalism and Left Politics* (Durham and London: Duke University Press, 2009).

37. Alain Badiou: *Greece and the Reinvention of politics* (London and New York: Verso, 2017).

38. Karl Marx: 'Critical Notes on the Article: The King of Prussia and Social Reform. By a Prussian', 1844; https://www.marxists.org/archive/marx/works/1844/08/07.htm

39. Cornelius Castoriadis: 'The Hungarian Source', in: *Telos*, no. 29, 1976, pp. 13-15.

40. Jacques Rancière: *Hatred of Democracy* (London: Verso, 2006).

41. Louis Althusser: 'Ideology and Ideological State Apparatuses (Notes towards an Investigation)', in *Lenin and Philosophy and Other Essays* (New York: Monthly Review Press, 1971), pp. 127-186.

42. Joel Olson: *The Abolition of White Democracy* (Minneapolis and London: University of Minnesota Press, 2004).

Zero Books

CULTURE, SOCIETY & POLITICS

Contemporary culture has eliminated the concept and public figure of the intellectual. A cretinous anti-intellectualism presides, cheer-led by hacks in the pay of multinational corporations who reassure their bored readers that there is no need to rouse themselves from their stupor. Zer0 Books knows that another kind of discourse – intellectual without being academic, popular without being populist – is not only possible: it is already flourishing. Zer0 is convinced that in the unthinking, blandly consensual culture in which we live, critical and engaged theoretical reflection is more important than ever before.

If you have enjoyed this book, why not tell other readers by posting a review on your preferred book site.

Recent bestsellers from Zero Books are:

In the Dust of This Planet
Horror of Philosophy vol. 1
Eugene Thacker
In the first of a series of three books on the Horror of
Philosophy, *In the Dust of This Planet* offers the genre of horror
as a way of thinking about the unthinkable.
Paperback: 978-1-84694-676-9 ebook: 978-1-78099-010-1

Capitalist Realism
Is there no alternative?
Mark Fisher
An analysis of the ways in which capitalism has presented itself
as the only realistic political-economic system.
Paperback: 978-1-84694-317-1 ebook: 978-1-78099-734-6

Rebel Rebel
Chris O'Leary
David Bowie: every single song. Everything you want to know,
everything you didn't know.
Paperback: 978-1-78099-244-0 ebook: 978-1-78099-713-1

Cartographies of the Absolute
Alberto Toscano, Jeff Kinkle
An aesthetics of the economy for the twenty-first century.
Paperback: 978-1-78099-275-4 ebook: 978-1-78279-973-3

Malign Velocities
Accelerationism and Capitalism
Benjamin Noys
Long listed for the Bread and Roses Prize 2015, *Malign Velocities* argues against the need for speed, tracking acceleration as the symptom of the ongoing crises of capitalism.
Paperback: 978-1-78279-300-7 ebook: 978-1-78279-299-4

Meat Market
Female Flesh under Capitalism
Laurie Penny
A feminist dissection of women's bodies as the fleshy fulcrum of capitalist cannibalism, whereby women are both consumers and consumed.
Paperback: 978-1-84694-521-2 ebook: 978-1-84694-782-7

Poor but Sexy
Culture Clashes in Europe East and West
Agata Pyzik
How the East stayed East and the West stayed West.
Paperback: 978-1-78099-394-2 ebook: 978-1-78099-395-9

Romeo and Juliet in Palestine
Teaching Under Occupation
Tom Sperlinger
Life in the West Bank, the nature of pedagogy and the role of a university under occupation.
Paperback: 978-1-78279-637-4 ebook: 978-1-78279-636-7

Readers of ebooks can buy or view any of these bestsellers by clicking on the live link in the title. Most titles are published in paperback and as an ebook. Paperbacks are available in traditional bookshops. Both print and ebook formats are available online.

Find more titles and sign up to our readers' newsletter at http://www.johnhuntpublishing.com/culture-and-politics

Follow us on Facebook
at https://www.facebook.com/ZeroBooks

and Twitter at https://twitter.com/Zer0Books